ervice

FISH AND SEAFOOD TO SHARE

First published in the United Kingdom in 2018 by
Pavilion
43 Great Ormond Street
London
WC1N 3HZ

ISBN: 978-1-911216-96-4

A CIP catalogue record for this book is available from the British Library.

10 9 8 7 6 5 4 3 2 1

Reproduction by Mission Productions, Hong Kong
Printed and bound by 1010 Printing International Ltd, China

This book can be ordered direct from the publisher at
www.pavilionbooks.com

FISH AND SEAFOOD
TO SHARE

RICK AND KATIE TOOGOOD

PAVILION

Contents

Foreword

The one thing all my favourite seafood restaurants have in common is that the chefs and owners understand seafood to such a level that it is evident in the way every fish is prepared and cooked. This is very much true of Prawn on the Lawn, a gem of a restaurant, run by my friends Rick and Katie. In their first restaurant, they didn't have cooking facilities, so light marinations, cures and raw fish is where these guys started. I loved the idea of a beautiful fish counter you could choose from and then have your selection simply prepared in front of you while you enjoyed a glass of wine – it was brilliant. I think it was due to this restricted kitchen set-up that Rick's food developed the character it has today.

Simple preparation and cooking of seafood takes some skill – the delicate textures of seafood really shine when the balance of flavours are just right. I love the hit of flavour of the POTL som tam crab salad – fresh, hot, fragrant, salty and cooling – a heady mouthful, especially with freshly picked crab that is somehow not overpowered by it all. It amounts to a plate prepared by a chef that has a real connection to what he is cooking – and that's Rick, he just gets it. So, sitting in any of their restaurants, with a whole crab, a plate of crispy fried seafood or some fresh oysters in front of you, is a joy, whether in the city or by the sea.

I think restaurants are a little about food and lot about other things too. When the balance of everything is right, the whole experience is wonderful. Most of the time you can't put your finger on what it is that makes it all work. I believe there is a sort of "umami" in certain restaurants, just as there is in the world of flavor – you love it, but you don't quite know what it is. I feel that sense of wholeness at POTL. The fish is the star of the room – it sits on the counter in all its glory letting you know what the place is all about, whilst the simple decor is personal and comfortable. A short wine list makes things easy, and the service from Katie and her team is good old-fashioned hospitality that makes you feel so welcome.

I really enjoy Rick's company; whenever a few of us foodie people make our annual trip to Italy to enjoy friendship and truffles, it's not long before we are discussing our mutual love of fish and seafood. Rick has always been somewhere new, or has a trip planned to far-off places, to do the hard research all restauranteurs have to do! And I always want to hear about it. I believe it's through travel, eating and life experience that we become better cooks and restaurateurs, and that is certainly true of POTL. The last time I ate there, I could sense Rick had been to Spain; crisp-fried whole red mullet, punchy romesco sauce and clams were on the menu, taking me right back to the sheer pleasure of simple seafood such as I first experienced myself in Barcelona many years ago.

I shall enjoy having POTL on my bookshelf – it's another great book to introduce the home cook to the joys of seafood cookery, to keep the experienced cook on the straight and narrow, and to remind us that it's all about the quality of seafood and simple preparations – deviate from this at your peril!

Mitch Tonks

Prawn on the Lawn

Our restaurant, Prawn on the Lawn, is built around a pretty clear ethos: Katie and I wanted to create a place where we would love to work, a place where our staff would love to serve great food and a place in which our customers would love to spend time. Moreover, we wanted to create an opportunity to share – share our knowledge and our passion for seafood, share where our ingredients come from, share our hospitality with each person that steps through the door, and ultimately, hopefully, share an enjoyable and memorable experience for all.

It feels like a lifetime ago when it all started. After completing a design degree at university, I was lost as to what route to take. A job in China made me realize that a life sat behind a desk wasn't for me. My mum came to the rescue, and asked me to write down the top three things I was most passionate about. Food came out on top, so off I went to work in a restaurant.

My first job was front of house in a restaurant near to where I grew up in Buckinghamshire – I learned a lot from that experience. Then I moved to London and continued working front of house, working my way up the ranks to become general manager of a fish restaurant, but I struggled with not being able to do things my way; my design degree was subconsciously at work, redesigning the dining experience. Along the way I met Katie – she was working in the music industry at various record labels in London. She was focused, driven and ambitious, with an equal desire to do things her way. 'My way' and 'her way' soon became our way!

I left my restaurant job and set about finding a site for us to start our own project. We decided that opening a full-blown restaurant was biting off more than we could chew – or afford! We had weeks of viewings all over north London (where we were living at the time) but nothing was suitable. A good mate of mine sent me a picture of an empty butcher's shop he cycled past. We met up with the landlord and couldn't believe our luck; he gave us the start we needed, a rent-free period with staged increases in rent. We'll be eternally grateful to him, for helping us get our dream off the ground.

We had a site, now for a name. The only option was to get a couple of bottles of wine, sit in the park, and see what happened. Katie jokingly blurted out 'Prawn on the Lawn', but it took a couple of weeks for us to realize that this was the perfect name.

When we started to work on the shop, we decided it was going to be a fishmonger's where you could sit and have a glass of wine with some oysters or maybe a cooked crab with some crusty bread. We wanted the styling to be reminiscent of a classic fishmonger's, but without the stainless steel, spray-the-walls-down feel to it. The shop was to have wine barrels and bar seating to encourage an informal vibe where people could share the space with others. We did everything on a budget: antique shops, reclaimed materials – you name it, we sourced it to get the dream started.

We enlisted the help of everyone we could think of. One of my brothers sorted out the bespoke fish counter, working through the night to help me build it. Next, we needed a logo and branding – its creation is a perfect example of the support we've had from family and friends. The typeface was done by my cousin, the illustration of the prawn in the deckchair by a friend, and it was all put together and styled by my best mate (and best man). Our website was kept up to date and run by my other brother. This sort of support has carried us through our entire Prawn on the Lawn life. We've had people dropping everything and throwing on a POTL shirt to wait tables, wash dishes and run food stalls for us.

At the beginning, I worked full time in our restaurant with one other member of staff. Katie kept her day job, working evenings and Saturdays front of house. Soon, we found that the 'eating in' side of what we were doing became far more popular than the fishmonger side, so we renovated the basement of the Islington site to fit in more covers. I started experimenting with some sharing-style dishes, using the cooking skills I learned from mum when I was growing up. However, I was restricted in what I could offer, as we only had a retail licence, so we weren't able to cook to order. It forced us to be more creative, which, looking back, helped shape what we do. Without being able to cook to order, I experimented with ceviches, pickles, cures and poaching fish. It was challenging at first, but I soon enjoyed coming up with new dishes every week; the key note of every dish was to allow the fish to shine through. Katie was then able to start at POTL full time. There was no going back now!

Right from the start we wanted to source from Cornwall. Partly for sentimental reasons, as we both used to go on holiday there, but primarily because of the amazing quality of the produce. I contacted Johnny Murt, who catches our crab and lobster in Padstow. He'd not shipped stuff up to London before, but we managed to sort out the logistics. It meant we had to start visiting Padstow regularly, obviously just to meet up with suppliers, nothing to do with the fact that we loved the place! The return journey became harder and harder. When a restaurant became available in the town, we didn't even think twice. We wanted to be nearer to where we sourced the produce and thought our concept would sit really well among the other great restaurants in the town, without directly competing with anyone. It also meant we now had a fully working kitchen to cook hot food.

So, now we have another opportunity to share in this book some of our favourite and the most popular recipes that we've served over the last four years. We never over-complicate our food – fresh ingredients are key. Fish is so versatile, and many of the recipes are interchangeable between different species. The best approach to take with these recipes is to get used to cooking them, and then start experimenting; mix and match the smaller tapas dishes and the larger sharing plates. The simplicity of the dishes enables you to come up with a cracker of a meal when entertaining. We've added in drinks pairings, too, to give you the complete experience in one book. Cook them up at home, on the beach, or in the garden on your barbecue. Get friends and family around, crack open a nice bottle of wine or a couple of beers, and share.

Rick and Katie

Sourcing Fish and Seafood

Where our ingredients come from has always been a vital part of what we do. As much as possible, we try to source our seafood as fresh and sustainable as it can be. It's tough these days to be a consumer who wants to purchase fish in a sustainable way – there has been so much conflicting information in the media about what you should and shouldn't buy. The truth is that there are constantly fluctuating quantities of different species all around our coast, so there's no golden rule.

Catching fish at sea is sustainable if the fishery takes into account the effect their activities are having on the ecosystem in which they operate. In a responsible fishery, there are enough fish left to swim away so that they can continue to reproduce in large numbers. So, by all means, catch fish, but always in moderation. A responsible fishing community will always ensure that their fishing causes as little damage to the seabed as possible and will minimize any by-catch. In addition, the fishery should be well organized and managed to ensure that the provenance of each fish can be traced.

To keep things simple, if every person tried as much as possible to buy fish from day boats, and varied what they ate, it would spread the load across all species. Don't be afraid to ask questions at the fishmonger's, from where the seafood was caught, or how it was caught, to what your fishmonger recommends that day. A good fishmonger should know the flavours and textures of the fish he or she is selling, and how best each type should be cooked. There are so many different and amazing fish available, with so many flavours, textures and uses – give them all a try!

Sterilizing Jars

Some of our recipes call for a sterilized jar to store pickled ginger (see p. 43), kalettes (see p. 54) or chutney (see p. 51) in order to extend the shelf life of the food. If your dishwasher has a very hot cycle, you can sterilize your jars and lids in that. Otherwise, we've added a couple of alternative methods below.

First, wash the jars and lids in hot, soapy water, making sure that there is no residue on them, and then rinse thoroughly in hot water. Heat the oven to 160°C fan/180°C/350°F/gas mark 4. Stand the jars, bottles and lids on the oven shelf and leave for 10 minutes to sterilize. Turn the oven off and keep them warm until ready to fill.

Alternatively, wash the jars and lids, then stand them right-side up on a wire rack in a large pan, making sure that they do not touch each other or the sides of the pan. Cover completely with water and then bring to the boil. Simmer for 10 minutes and then remove from the water and stand upside down on a clean, thick cloth to drain. Dry completely in a preheated oven at 90°C fan/110°C/225°F/gas mark ¼, right-side up on a baking sheet for about 15 minutes. They can be kept warm in the oven until required.

Key Marinades and Recipes

In this section, you will find a collection of basic recipes that can be used in a wide variety of ways, and that suit many different types of seafood. We base our menu on the day's catch, which means we have to be very flexible — these key recipes enable us to do that. Master these recipes and you can make anything from soups to marinated fish and roasted shellfish. I would encourage you to play around with different species of fish and shellfish with these recipes. To a certain extent, this ethos can be carried through the whole book — don't be afraid to experiment.

Vietnamese Marinade

This is one of the most versatile recipes in the book. It can be used across the whole spectrum of fish and shellfish species, both as a marinade and as a dipping sauce. Whilst on our honeymoon in Vietnam, Katie and I went on a motorbike tour of seafood restaurants around Ho Chi Minh City. We enjoyed one particularly amazing dip with some barbecued prawns. When we returned, I tried to recreate it and hope I've done it justice. This makes quite a lot of marinade, but any extra can be kept for up to 3 days in the fridge, or frozen for later use.

Put all the ingredients into a food processor or blender and blitz until as smooth as possible. Don't worry if it looks a little 'bitty', as it will soften down during the cooking process. You now have the basis for an array of different recipes.

Makes about 150ml/5fl oz/scant ⅔ cup (enough dipping sauce for 10)

2 garlic cloves, peeled
a handful of coriander (cilantro), stalks and all
5 kaffir lime leaves
1 thumb-sized piece of fresh ginger, peeled
1 birdseye chilli, roughly chopped
2 lemongrass stalks, topped and tailed, roughly chopped
a splash of Thai fish sauce (nam pla)
juice of 2 limes
50 ml/1¾ fl oz/scant ¼ cup extra-virgin olive oil

Soy Marinade

For Katie's 30th birthday celebrations, a big crowd of us went to stay in an amazing house in Oxfordshire. I'd been playing around with this recipe for a couple of weeks. Since I was in charge of the food and knew that Katie was a massive fan of scallops, I decided to unleash it on the 20-strong group. I cooked the scallops over a fire pit and it went down a storm. I've since tried this marinade in loads of other ways – as a dip as well as a marinade (see the Squid with Tenderstem Broccoli, p. 44, or the Salmon Sashimi, p. 43). It's another versatile recipe to keep up your sleeve.

Makes about 100 ml/3½ fl oz/7 tbsp

1 tbsp sesame oil
3 tbsp soy sauce
1 tsp finely chopped garlic
1 tsp finely chopped fresh ginger
juice of ½ lemon

Combine all the ingredients and job done!

Extra-virgin Olive Oil and Lemon Dressing

These two ingredients can transform fish or shellfish from just average into something to remember. It's a combination I remember from sailing around Greece with my parents.

We're known for keeping things simple, but even I wasn't sure about adding this to the book! Please try it though.

The ratio:
70% extra-virgin olive oil (the best you can buy)
30% freshly squeezed lemon juice

Whisk together and that's it!

Nam Jim Dipping Sauce

One of our first ever holidays together was in Thailand. Katie, being obsessed with the country, planned the whole thing. Of all the amazing things we ate, this was one of the key recipes I took from the experience. The name *nam jim* is rather generic in Thailand and covers a variety of sauces, but this one I've tweaked and it works in a variety of ways: as a marinade, as a sauce and as a dip.

Mix all the ingredients together in a bowl and there you go! Purists would say that palm sugar ought to be added, but I prefer to let the natural sweetness of the seafood add this element.

Makes about 6 tbsp (enough dipping sauce for 4)

1 tbsp Thai fish sauce (nam pla)
1 red chilli, deseeded and finely sliced
2 tsp finely chopped fresh ginger
juice of 2 limes

Smoked Paprika Dip

Another great dip for cold cooked shellfish, this also works perfectly with fish tempura.

Just mix it up.

Serves 4

4 tbsp crème fraîche
½ tsp smoked paprika (pimentón) (the hotter the better)
1 tsp lemon juice
a pinch of sea salt and freshly ground black pepper

Garlic Crème Fraîche

I use crème fraîche as an alternative to mayo. At home, when I was growing up, we used to put it with everything and it always seemed to taste good. This is a garlicky version – we use it in the restaurant with a wide variety of seafood, from smoked salmon to crab, or as a dip for all the different crustaceans on a fruits de mer platter.

Serves 4

4 tbsp crème fraîche
½ tsp garlic paste (shop-bought)
2 spring onions (scallions), finely sliced
1 tsp lemon juice
a pinch of sea salt and freshly ground black pepper

Mix all the ingredients together and get dipping!

Shallot Vinegar

A classic accompaniment to oysters; red wine vinegar is traditionally used, but you could also experiment with different flavoured vinegars.

Serves 4

100 ml/3½ fl oz/7 tbsp good-quality red wine vinegar
1 banana shallot, finely chopped

Combine the ingredients and drizzle over fresh oysters.

Cold Tapas

These dishes are our roots. When we first opened, we didn't have a hot food licence, so all our dishes were served cold. The key to this section is preparation. If you're putting on a spread for friends and family, these recipes are all perfect to throw together at the last minute, as long as you've prepared all the components beforehand. The Mackerel Pâté (see p. 51), in particular, is a real crowd pleaser.

Prawn on the Lawn

This is the first ever dish we served in the restaurant. We had the name and the shop, so then we needed a dish that wasn't too gimmicky. Right from the off, this reflected all the other dishes that followed – bags of flavour, simple to make, it packs a punch and is a true classic.

Scoop the flesh from the avocados into a mixing bowl. Add 2 tbsp of lime juice and mash. Season with salt and pepper, to taste. This mix can be left in the fridge until needed; just leave an avocado stone in the mix and cover in cling film (plastic wrap) and it won't turn brown.

Finely chop the coriander, reserving a few leaves for garnish.

Toast the soda bread, then spoon the avocado mix equally over the slices. Place 3 cooked prawns on each slice. Sprinkle the chilli over the prawns, pour 1 tbsp of the remaining lime juice on top of each slice and sprinkle over the chopped coriander.

Garnish with the reserved coriander, or use the micro-coriander leaves if you have them. Serve immediately, with a wedge of lime.

Serves 4

2 ready-to-eat avocados, Hass are best
6 tbsp lime juice
sea salt and freshly ground black pepper
3–4 sprigs of coriander (cilantro)
4 slices of soda bread (see p. 156)
12 cooked king prawns (jumbo shrimp), peeled and deveined (you can buy raw if you prefer and cook them in boiling lightly salted water for 1–2 minutes)
1 fresh red chilli, deseeded and finely diced
micro-coriander (cilantro), to garnish (if available)
1 lime, quartered, to serve

Pairs well with
Verdejo
Spanish fizz

Smoked Salmon with Shallots, Capers and Garlic Crème Fraîche

Smoking is a traditional way of preserving fish, and in recent years there have been numerous independent smokehouses opening up, so the technique has seen a real resurgence. Try and hunt down a smokery near you, as each one will have a distinct flavour depending on their own curing recipe and the wood they choose to smoke the fish with.

This is a really simple recipe, but then you don't want anything too OTT, as you'd distract from the flavour of the smoked salmon.

Lay the salmon on the serving dish, with a pile of the shallots and capers heaped next to it, and the lemon wedges on the side. Add a ramekin of garlic crème fraîche and serve with the slices of toasted soda or rye bread.

Serves 4

350 g/12 oz smoked salmon, ideally cut vertically (the traditional Scandinavian way)
2 banana shallots, finely diced
3 tbsp capers
lemon wedges
1 quantity Garlic Crème Fraîche (see p. 27)
slices of soda bread (see p. 156) or rye bread, toasted

Pairs well with
Sancerre

Herring Rollmops

Rollmops are such a 'Marmite' dish: some people hate them, but I love them! My auntie is Swedish – on trips over to see my cousins I'd always gorge on all sorts of pickled fish, packed full of dill. Back then, rollmops seemed like an impossible thing to make by yourself; however, they're remarkably simple, as long as you allow at least three days' pickling time.

Lay the herring fillets out on a chopping board, skin-side down, and sprinkle over the chopped dill.

Carefully roll the fillets up, as tightly as possible, and fasten in place by piercing each roll with a cocktail stick. Transfer to a container, making sure the rollmops don't have much space around them otherwise they won't stay submerged.

Add all the pickling ingredients to a saucepan and bring to the boil, then remove from the heat and leave until cool.

Once the pickling mixture is cool, pour it over the rolled herrings, making sure they are all covered. Cover in cling film (plastic wrap) and store in the fridge for at least 3 days.

To serve, place the rollmops on a serving dish, drizzle with a little pickling liquor, and put a ramekin of garlic crème fraîche and some rye bread on the side.

Serves 4

8 herring fillets, pin bones removed
a bunch of dill, finely chopped
8 cocktail sticks

For the pickling mixture:
1 shallot, finely chopped
2 garlic cloves, crushed
a pinch of mustard seeds
3 bay leaves
a pinch of black peppercorns
grated zest of 1 orange
1 tbsp brown sugar
250 ml/9 fl oz/1 cup white wine vinegar
125 ml/4 fl oz/½ cup dry white wine

1 quantity Garlic Crème Fraîche (see p. 27), to serve
4–8 slices of rye bread, to serve

Pairs well with
Lager
Aquavit

Skate Wing with Baby Gem and Smoked Anchovy Dressing

Skate, or ray as it's also known, is more often than not served the classic way with black butter and capers. Here, it's poached and tossed through a simple salad. The smoked anchovy dressing is the key to getting bags of flavour.

Bring a saucepan of lightly salted water to a simmer and add the bay leaves, the 2 crushed garlic cloves and the peppercorns. Gently lower the fish into the water and poach for 7 minutes.

Using a fish slice or slotted spoon, carefully remove the fish from the pan onto a plate – don't worry if it breaks up. While it is still warm, flake the flesh into small pieces – it should naturally split along the fibres. Leave to cool.

Into a food processor or blender, add the anchovies, the remaining garlic clove, the white wine vinegar and lemon juice, and blend, while slowly adding in the olive oil.

Both stages of this recipe can be done the day before, but be sure to keep the skate in the fridge and remove 10 minutes before using, to allow it to come to room temperature.

Mix the shredded lettuce with the skate, shallots, capers and dressing and mix thoroughly. Transfer to a serving plate and sprinkle with the chives and some sea salt.

Serves 4

sea salt
2 bay leaves
3 garlic cloves, peeled – 2 crushed and 1 left whole
a pinch of whole black peppercorns
300 g/10½ oz skate (ray) wing, bone and cartilage removed (your fishmonger can do this for you)

For the dressing:
½ a 30 g/1 oz tin of smoked anchovies (15 g/½ oz drained weight)
a generous splash of white wine vinegar
juice of ½ a lemon
100 ml/3½ fl oz/7 tbsp extra-virgin olive oil

2 baby gem (Boston) lettuces, finely shredded (the finer the better)
2 shallots, finely sliced
a small handful of capers
a small bunch of chives, finely chopped

Pairs well with
Muscadet

Oysters 3 Ways

This is not one for oyster purists, but it perfectly reflects POTL's obsession with flavour. When buying oysters from your fishmonger, ensure that the oysters are firmly closed and do not feel hollow. They should have some weight to them – this means they still have liquid inside, ensuring they are in great shape. Rock (Pacific) oysters are better than natives for this.

Note: The Pickled Cucumber and Dill Dressing should ideally be made 1–2 days in advance.

Mix the diced cucumber with the white wine vinegar. Add the chopped dill with a pinch of sugar and mix well. Store in the fridge until needed.

Shuck (open and detatch from their shells) the oysters and place on crushed ice (or a pile of sea salt) on a serving platter – we use a round metal tray in the restaurant.
For the first 4 oysters, sprinkle the desiccated coconut over equally, then add the chilli, followed by the lime juice, and garnish each with a coriander leaf.

For the next 4 oysters, dollop about ½ tsp crème fraîche on each, then add the same amount of keta caviar, finishing off with a good grinding of black pepper.

For the final 4 oysters, spoon over the pickled cucumber dressing and garnish with a dill leaf from the remaining sprig. Serve immediately.

Serves 4

12 oysters
crushed ice or a quantity of sea salt, for presentation

Pickled Cucumber and Dill Dressing:
¼ cucumber, peeled, deseeded if large and watery, and finely diced
25 ml/1 fl oz/scant 2 tbsp white wine vinegar
4 sprigs of dill, leaves only, roughly chopped, plus 1 sprig for garnish
a pinch of caster (superfine) sugar

Coconut, Chilli and Lime Dressing:
4 tsp desiccated (dried grated) coconut
2 fresh red chillies, finely diced
4 tsp lime juice
4 coriander (cilantro) leaves

Crème Fraîche, Keta Caviar and Black Pepper Dressing:
2 tsp crème fraîche
2 tsp keta caviar (salmon roe)
cracked black pepper

Pairs well with
English fizz

Whilst on our travels around Thailand we ate many *som tam*, freshly made in front of us on the streets of the towns and cities, as well as on the beach. It became Katie's favourite dish and something I had to recreate at home. This is a simplified, less spicy version, but it still packs a punch, combining the typical salty, sweet, sour and spicy flavours of the region. Here, I've used freshly picked crab meat, but you could also use diced prawns (shrimp) or even lobster if you want to make it extra fancy!

Using a mandolin, slice the carrots and green papaya into thin matchsticks. Place in a mixing bowl, add the garlic and pour over the nam jim dipping sauce. Mix thoroughly, cover the bowl with cling film (plastic wrap) and store in the fridge for at least 1 hour to allow the flavours to infuse.

When ready to serve, remove the bowl from the fridge and add the mint, coriander, squashed tomatoes, spring onions, and chilli (if using). Mix thoroughly. Transfer to a serving plate, forming a small pile, and top with the crab meat. Sprinkle with the toasted peanuts and serve.

Serves 4

2 large carrots, peeled
1 small to medium green (unripe) papaya, peeled (or green beans, finely sliced)
2 tsp finely chopped garlic
6 tbsp Nam Jim Dipping Sauce (see p. 26)
a small handful of mint leaves
a small handful of coriander (cilantro) leaves
8 cherry tomatoes, halved (or quartered, if large) and squashed slightly
2 spring onions (scallions), finely sliced
1 fresh red chilli, deseeded and finely sliced (optional)
150 g/5½ oz white crab meat (unpasteurized)
a handful of toasted peanuts, crushed

Crab Som Tam Salad

Pairs well with
Verdejo

Salmon Sashimi with Soy, Mooli and Pickled Ginger

Salmon and soy are a match made in heaven. Take some time to source your fish as sustainably as possible and ask your fishmonger for sashimi-grade salmon. Have a go at slicing it yourself, but if you don't feel confident, just ask your fishmonger to do it for you – that's what we're here for! You will need to start at least the day before you want to serve, to make the pickled ginger.

For the pickled ginger, add the slices of ginger to a bowl, sprinkle with the salt and mix thoroughly. Set to one side for 30 minutes. Squeeze any excess liquid from the ginger and transfer to a sterilized jar (see p. 20).

In a small saucepan set over a low-medium heat, gently heat the rice wine vinegar, water and sugar, until the sugar has dissolved. Turn the heat up and bring to the boil. As soon as it has come to the boil, carefully pour the mixture over the ginger slices and seal the jar. Place in the fridge for at least 24 hours.

If your salmon hasn't already been sliced, cut vertically into 1-cm/ ½-in slices, cover in cling film (plastic wrap) and store in the fridge until needed.

To serve, place the salmon slices on a serving plate, with a tangle of mooli and spring onion on the side. Bring to the table with a ramekin of the soy marinade and a pile of pickled ginger, for guests to serve themselves.

Serves 4

For the pickled ginger:
100 g/3½ oz fresh ginger, peeled and cut into thin slices
1 tsp sea salt
50 ml/1½ fl oz/3½ tbsp rice wine vinegar
50 ml/1½ fl oz/3½ tbsp water
40 g/1½ oz/3 tbsp caster (superfine) sugar

300 g/10½ oz sashimi-grade salmon, skin removed, sliced vertically into 1-cm/½-in slices

½ a mooli (daikon), peeled and cut into matchsticks (enough for a small handful) (alternatively use radishes)
2 spring onions (scallions), finely sliced into strips

1 quantity Soy Marinade (see p. 24)

Pairs well with
A full-bodied white, such as Sancerre

When POTL Islington began the transition from primarily being a fishmonger to becoming a destination to eat super-fresh seafood tapas, this was one of the first dishes on the menu. The components can all be made up in advance and then assembled at the last minute, making it a great dinner party dish. It's also really healthy.

If the tentacles of your squid are thick, cut them lengthways to make them thinner, so they cook evenly.

Bring a saucepan of lightly salted water to the boil. Add the squid and cook for 1½ minutes. Take a piece out to check after 1 minute: if tender, remove the pan from the heat; if not, then cook for a bit longer.

Drain the squid into a colander, and cover with ice to stop the cooking process.

In a separate saucepan, bring more lightly salted water to the boil and add the broccoli. Cook for 1–2 minutes, until tender. Drain and plunge into a bowl of ice-cold water to stop the cooking process. Drain again, and store in the fridge, along with the squid, until needed.

When ready to serve, add the squid and broccoli to a mixing bowl and mix in all the remaining ingredients, except the poppy seeds, making sure they are well combined. Transfer to a serving plate and form a neat pile. Sprinkle with poppy seeds and serve.

Serves 4

300 g/10½ oz squid, cleaned and cut into rings, including the wings and tentacles
sea salt, to salt the cooking water
ice, for cooling
200 g/7 oz tenderstem broccoli (broccolini)
6 tbsp Soy Marinade (see p. 24)
juice of 2 lemons
a small handful of mint leaves
2 fresh red chillies, finely sliced
3 spring onions (scallions), finely sliced
2 pinches of poppy seeds

Squid with Tenderstem Broccoli and Soy Marinade

Pairs well with
IPA
Albariño

Burrata with Chicory, Anchovies and Almonds

Down the road from our Islington restaurant, we are lucky to have an amazing Italian restaurant called Trullo. It was here that Katie and I first had burrata on the recommendation of the manager, and now good friend, Sam James. I've been obsessed ever since. For me, the key is using the best olive oil you can find – it really makes all the difference.

Heat a good glug of olive oil in a frying pan (skillet) over a medium heat. Season the chicory with salt and add to the frying pan with a splash of the white wine vinegar, then cover with a lid. After a minute, remove the lid and flip the chicory over and fry for a further minute.

Place the chicory on a serving plate. Remove the burrata from its packaging and pat dry with paper towels. Place on top of the chicory and gently break open the cheeses. Pour over a generous amount of extra-virgin olive oil and scatter over the anchovies and flaked almonds.

Serves 4

olive oil, for frying
3 red chicory (radicchio), split lengthways
sea salt, to taste
a splash of sweet white wine vinegar
2 burrata or burratina (use buffalo mozzarella if not available)
a generous glug of extra-virgin olive oil
5 salted anchovies
a small handful of flaked almonds

Pairs well with
Grolleau Gris

Smoked Mackerel Pâté

I usually find mackerel pâté pretty boring. So when we put it on the menu in the early days of the restaurant, I wanted to tart it up a bit. Beetroot adds colour and sweetness and the horseradish adds a bit of bite. If you're in a rush, you can always use a bought chutney, but if you have time, it's nice to make your own.

Make the chutney at least a week in advance. It will keep for a few weeks and works really well with cheese or with cold meats, as well as in sandwiches.

Combine all the chutney ingredients in a saucepan. Top up with water, until it just reaches the level of the ingredients. Bring up to a simmer and cook for about 3 hours over a very low heat, stirring at least every 30 minutes, until the ingredients soften, darken and the liquid has evaporated. You will need to stir more frequently the drier the mixture gets. Set aside to cool. You can transfer it to a sterilized jar (see p. 20), if wished. It will keep for 2–3 weeks in the fridge.

For the pâté, flake the mackerel fillets into a mixing bowl and add the rest of the ingredients, stirring vigorously with a fork. Don't mix it in a blender, as you would lose the texture. Once fully combined, transfer to a serving bowl and serve with the chutney and some bread.

The pâté will keep for up to 1 week in the fridge in a lidded container.

Serves 4

For the chutney:
2 large red onions, finely sliced
1 thumb-sized piece of fresh ginger, peeled and finely chopped
2 garlic cloves, finely chopped
3 cooked beetroot (beets), roughly chopped
½ tsp Chinese five spice
4 tbsp soft light brown sugar
100 ml/3½ fl oz/7 tbsp red wine vinegar
100 ml/3½ fl oz/7 tbsp red wine

For the pâté:
4 fillets of smoked mackerel, skin and pin bones removed
2 cooked beetroot (beets) (not the ones in vinegar), cut into small cubes
small handful of parsley, finely chopped
1 tbsp freshly grated horseradish
1 garlic clove, finely chopped
juice of ½ a lemon
2 tbsp crème fraîche

sourdough or soda bread (see p. 156), to serve

Pairs well with
A Provençal rosé
A chilled light red, such as Gamay

Raw Carabineros Prawns with Basil Oil and Orange Zest

If you haven't tried these prawns yet, you haven't lived! They taste incredible – super sweet – and sucking the heads gives a huge amount of flavour. Featured most prominently on menus in Spain and Portugal, they're typically grilled very simply. This recipe adds a little something extra, without detracting from the amazing flavour.

To make the basil oil, bring a saucepan of lightly salted water to the boil. Plunge the basil leaves into the water for 30 seconds, then remove with a slotted spoon straight into a bowl of iced water. Squeeze out any excess water from the basil and transfer to a small blender or spice grinder. Add the olive oil and blend for 2–3 minutes. Pour into a small saucepan, cover and refrigerate for a few hours. After this time, remove from the fridge and gently heat the oil to bring it back to liquid form. Strain through a fine sieve and set aside until ready to use.

Carefully peel the shells from the body of the prawns, leaving the heads attached. Arrange on a serving plate and drizzle with the basil oil. Sprinkle the orange zest over the top and season the prawns with a little sea salt before serving.

Serves 4

For the basil oil:
a small handful of basil leaves
100 ml/3½ fl oz/7 tbsp light
    olive oil

For the prawns:
12 raw sashimi-grade carabineros
    prawns (jumbo shrimp)
zest of 1 orange
sea salt

Pairs well with
A dry sherry, such as Manzanilla Fino

Whipped Cod's Roe with Pickled Kalettes

I love smoked cod's roe – it's so under-used as an ingredient, but is well worth having on the table for everyone to have a dip. My good friend Mitch Tonks gave me a great bit of advice: don't worry too much about removing all the skin, that's where a lot of the smoky flavour is. Kalettes, also known as flower sprouts, are a hybrid of a sprout and kale and they have become very fashionable recently, but we've been buying them from our local producer, Padstow Kitchen Garden, for years. They work so well when pickled and cut through the smokiness of the roe.

For the pickled kalettes, place the kalettes in a sterilized sealable jar (see p. 20). Add the remaining ingredients to a saucepan and bring to the boil. Simmer for 1 minute, then carefully pour the mixture over the kalettes and seal the jar. Leave in the fridge for at least 10 hours before serving. They can be kept for up to 1 month in the fridge.

For the whipped cod's roe, remove any thick veins from the skin-like sac with a sharp knife, and place the roe into a food processor or blender. Add the lemon juice, zest and garlic, and blend, while slowly adding the olive oil. Transfer the mixture to a mixing bowl and add the crème fraîche. Using a balloon whisk, whip the mixture to a light texture.

Spoon the mixture into a serving bowl and create a well in the middle. Halve 8–10 of the pickled kalettes and place in the well, then sprinkle with the cucumber, sun-dried tomato, salt and pepper. Serve with flatbread or soda bread.

Serves 4

For the pickled kalettes:
2 large handfuls of kalettes
75 ml/2½ fl oz/5 tbsp white wine
75 ml/2½ fl oz/5 tbsp white wine vinegar
75 ml/2½ fl oz/5 tbsp water
75 g/2½ oz/6 tbsp caster (superfine) sugar
1 sprig of thyme
2 garlic cloves, crushed

For the whipped cod's roe:
200 g/7 oz smoked cod's roe
juice and zest of 1 lemon
2 garlic cloves
150 ml/5 fl oz/scant ⅔ cup light olive oil
200 ml/7 fl oz/scant 1 cup crème fraîche

For the garnish:
thumb-sized length of cucumber, finely cubed
5 sun-dried tomatoes, roughly chopped
2 pinches of sea salt and freshly ground black pepper

flatbread or soda bread (see p. 156), to serve

Pairs well with
A light dry rosé from the Loire Valley or Provence

Sea Trout Ceviche with Avocado

This is a super-simple version of a ceviche. Katie and I went on a fishing trip off the Yucatán Peninsula, Mexico, close to an island called Holbox. As with all fishing trips, I caught nothing, although Katie fortunately caught a few sea trout. We pulled up to a deserted island where I filleted the fish and our fisherman made this very dish for us, there and then. If you can't find sea trout, salmon makes a good alternative.

———————————————

In a mixing bowl, place the sea trout, red onion, chopped coriander, half the chilli, half the lime juice and a few pinches of salt and pepper. Mix thoroughly and allow to marinate for around 5 minutes, so that the acidity of the lime 'cooks' the fish.

Turn the mixture into a serving dish. Place the avocado on top and garnish with the reserved coriander.

In a separate bowl, combine the remaining lime juice and chilli. Add a generous pinch of salt and pepper and stir. Serve the ceviche with the extra lime juice on the side for those who would like an extra chilli kick to the dish.

Serves 4

350 g/12 oz sashimi-grade sea trout, skinned and diced into 2-cm/¾-in cubes
1 medium red onion, finely diced
1 medium bunch of coriander (cilantro), finely chopped, reserving a few leaves for garnish
2 fresh red chillies (habanero ideally), finely sliced
juice of 8 limes
sea salt and freshly ground black pepper
1 avocado, diced

Pairs well with
Sparkling white wine

Martin Morales, owner of the amazing Ceviche restaurants, really opened my eyes to the process of 'cooking' fish by using citrus. It was just before we opened the Islington branch of POTL that Katie and I ate at his awesome restaurant on Frith Street, London. For us, not having any cooking facilities in the original POTL, this was the perfect way to enhance the flavours of our fresh fish and shellfish without using any heat.

'Tiger's milk' is the Peruvian term for the citrus-based marinade that cures the seafood in a ceviche. In Peru, this invigorating potion is often served in a small glass alongside the ceviche and is believed to be a hangover cure as well as an aphrodisiac.

Using a food processor or blender, blitz all the ingredients for the tiger's milk thoroughly. Pass through a sieve, to remove the pulp, and set the liquid to one side.

Lay the scallop slices out on a serving plate and pour the tiger's milk evenly over the top, making sure each slice is covered. Drizzle the passion fruit seeds over (try to get roughly 1–2 passion fruit seeds on each scallop), sprinkle with the red chilli and garnish with the coriander leaves. Serve immediately.

Serves 4

For the tiger's milk:
1 stick of celery, roughly chopped
1 garlic clove
1 fresh green chilli
juice of 3 small limes
½ a thumb-sized piece of fresh ginger, peeled

9 sustainably sourced scallops, roes removed, thinly sliced into discs
seeds of 1 passion fruit
1 fresh red chilli, deseeded and finely diced
a handful of coriander (cilantro) leaves (use micro-coriander, if you can find it)

Scallop Ceviche

Pairs well with
Champagne
Sparkling Albariño

Octopus Carpaccio

Octopus is one of those species that people are often too frightened to cook. A definite crowd pleaser, this recipe ensures a super-tender meat and, once mastered, you can add your own twists by mixing up different herbs to garnish. Start the day before you want to serve.

In a large stockpot or saucepan, big enough to hold the octopuses, heat a splash of olive oil over a low heat. Add the garlic and cook for about 3 minutes, until softened. Add the octopus and the bay leaves, then fill with enough boiling water to cover the octopus. Bring to a simmer, then cover and cook for 1½ hours. After this time, you can check if the octopus is cooked by squeezing the thickest part of one of the tentacles with tongs. If it feels soft, with little resistance, it's done. The octopus will be very tender and delicate, so carefully remove from the pot, transfer to a chopping board, and set aside.

Lay out 2 large sheets of cling film (plastic wrap), one on top of the other, on your work surface.

While the cooked octopus is still warm, remove each tentacle from the body and lay them lengthways alongside each other in the middle of the sheets of cling film. Lift the cling film over the tentacles and tightly roll into a sausage shape. Pierce a few holes in the cling film, to allow air to escape, then simultaneously twist the cling film at each end to tighten into a firm roll. Wrap in one more layer of cling film, ensuring that the ends are completely sealed. Place in the fridge overnight, or for at least 12 hours, to cool and set. The natural gelatine released from the octopus will set the tentacles together.

Remove from the fridge just before serving. Remove the cling film layers – the sausage shape will hold, but act fast. Lay the sausage on its side on a chopping board and, using a sharp knife, carefully cut thin slices to give you perfect rounds of tender octopus. Lay the slices out on your serving plate/s, drizzle with a little white balsamic vinegar and olive oil, and finally sprinkle with a little salt, parsley, chilli and chives, to garnish. Serve immediately.

Serves 4

a splash of olive oil
3 garlic cloves, crushed
2 whole Mediterranean octopuses, around 2 kg/4 lb 8 oz each, cleaned (frozen Mediterranean octopuses are usually already cleaned. Avoid English octopuses – they are too difficult to cook)
4 bay leaves

To garnish:
a drizzle of white balsamic vinegar or sherry vinegar
a drizzle of good-quality extra-virgin olive oil
sea salt flakes, to taste
2 sprigs of parsley, leaves only, finely chopped
2 fresh red chillies, deseeded and finely diced
4 chives, finely sliced

Pairs well with
Albariño

Seared Tuna with Chilli, Soy and Mirin

Originally, Prawn on the Lawn was only meant to be an oyster bar attached to a fishmonger. We had our Scallop Ceviche (p. 58) and Prawn on the Lawn (p. 30) dishes on from the start, but when customers flocked for the dining side of the concept, I had to start thinking of new recipes. We were sourcing incredible line-caught yellowfin tuna at the time, and it seemed the perfect fish to use – it didn't need to be cooked, as it was sashimi-grade. We brought in a tiny, single induction hob, so that we could sear the fish a little, and it's been on the menu ever since!

You can ask your fishmonger to cut the tuna to size, so that you have chunks that are roughly 10-cm/4-in thick, by 20-cm/8-in long.

Heat a large, non-stick frying pan (skillet) over a medium heat and add a drizzle of olive oil. Place the tuna in the pan carefully. As the meat cooks it will change from a deep red to a grey colour and you only want to see it colour just a few millimetres in (which will take about 20 seconds). Roll the tuna over and repeat the process until all the sides are seared. The ends should remain uncooked.

Remove from the pan to a plate and allow to cool. Store in the fridge for at least 30 minutes, for the tuna to firm up.

Using a sharp knife, cut the tuna loin into roughly 1-cm/½-in thick slices. Fan the slices out on a serving plate and sprinkle over the chilli, spring onion and coriander. In a small dish, mix the soy sauce and mirin together and place next to the tuna, to serve. You can dip the tuna slices into it, or pour it all over the tuna, it's up to you!

Serves 4

olive oil, for searing
500 g/1 lb 2 oz sashimi-grade, line-caught tuna loin
2 fresh red chillies, deseeded and finely diced
4 spring onions (scallions), finely sliced
a small bunch of coriander (cilantro), leaves only, finely chopped, or micro-coriander
75 ml/2½ fl oz/5 tbsp soy sauce
2 tbsp mirin (rice wine vinegar)

Pairs well with
Chinon
Pinot Noir

Langoustines are an incredible species; their flavour is super sweet. There's no getting away from the fact that the fresher they are, the better they taste, so avoid previously frozen and opt for live langoustines – they also have a much firmer texture. In this recipe, the extra ingredients are there to enhance the flavour, but it is the langoustines that do the talking. This recipe can be served cold or hot.

———————————————

If you are buying ready-cooked langoustines, ensure that they haven't been previously frozen, as the meat can be quite mushy. The best option is to buy them live and either boil in salted water for 2 minutes or, if you can handle it, split them in half live before cooking them. To do this, place the point of a sharp knife on the cross on the top of the langoustine's head. Cut firmly down through the head to split. Turn the langoustine, hold firmly and continue cutting through the centre line, down the full length

of the body. Open out, pull out the 'sandbox', near the head, and devein.

If the langoustines were previously cooked, they can be served right away. Lay the split langoustines on a serving plate, meat-side up, place a sprig of thyme on each half and drizzle with olive oil. Serve with the lemon halves (charred in a hot pan, if wished). Taste before seasoning with salt, as they may not need it.

If you want to serve them hot, follow these further steps.

Heat a little olive oil in a frying pan (skillet) over a medium-high heat. Sprinkle the langoustines with the thyme sprigs and place in the pan, meat-side down, ensuring they're sitting on top of the thyme sprigs. Add the lemon halves to the pan, cut-side down. Fry for 1 minute, then turn the langoustines over and fry for a further 30 seconds. Transfer to a serving plate, sprinkle a little sea salt over them and garnish with the charred lemon halves.

Serves 4

16 small to medium or 8 large langoustines
32 sprigs of fresh thyme or 16 if only using 8 langoustines,
extra-virgin olive oil, for drizzling
1 lemon, halved
sea salt, to taste

Split Langoustines with Thyme and Olive Oil

Pairs well with
Prosecco
A dry sherry, such as Manzanilla
Fino

Beetroot-cured Salmon with Tarragon Ricotta, Pickled Cucumber and Dill

Curing was a method of preserving fish and meat back in the days when fridges weren't around. It's a great way of changing the texture and adding a huge amount of flavour to the fish, especially when other ingredients are introduced to the curing process. Beetroot adds a sweet, earthy taste as well as a splash of purple to the salmon.

Place the salmon fillet in a non-reactive (glass, ceramic or stainless steel) container.

Thoroughly mix the salt, sugar, beetroot, lemon zest and juice together. Pour over the salmon fillet, cover with cling film (plastic wrap) and refrigerate for 8 hours.

Once the salmon has firmed up, remove from the fridge, wash off the curing salt and pat dry with paper towels. Cut the salmon vertically into 1-cm/½-in slices (first cut down to the skin, then slice horizontally, to remove each slice cleanly from the skin) and lay on a serving plate.

Thoroughly mix the pickled cucumber ingredients together and pile next to the salmon. Do the same with the tarragon ricotta ingredients. Serve with slices of rye or soda bread.

Serves 4

300 g/10½ oz fresh salmon fillet, skin on
50 g/1¾ oz/3 heaped tbsp table salt
50 g/1¾ oz/3 heaped tbsp caster (superfine) sugar
2 cooked beetroot (beet), finely chopped
zest and juice of 1 small lemon

For the pickled cucumber:
½ cucumber, peeled and cut into 1-cm/½-in cubes
a small handful of chopped dill
a good splash of white wine vinegar

For the tarragon ricotta:
100 g/3½ oz ricotta
4 sprigs of tarragon, leaves only, finely chopped
zest of 1 lemon

rye bread or soda bread (see p. 156), to serve

Pairs well with Prosecco

Razor Clams with Nam Jim, Coconut and Passion Fruit

Whilst out in Thailand, I became obsessed with fish sauce – it has an incredible flavour when mixed with other classic Asian ingredients such as the ginger and lime juice in the nam jim dipping sauce. In this recipe it really brings out the fresh meatiness of the clams.

Razor clams are my favourite of this family of shellfish. They should be bought live from the fishmonger – look for clams that are tightly closed (they might hang out of the end of the shell, but should instantly retract when touched). Although there's a little work involved to clean the clams, the dish can be prepared in advance – you can cook and prepare the meat of the razor clams the day before and store, covered, in the fridge. It's a great dish for entertaining – it's packed with flavour and looks amazing on the plate.

Place the razor clams in a bowl, fill it with water to submerge them completely, and leave in the fridge for 15 minutes. This will remove any sand or grit in the meat. Drain.

Heat a large, lidded saucepan over a medium-high heat. When hot, add the razor clams and 50 ml/ 1½ fl oz/3½ tbsp of water and quickly cover with the lid. Steam for about 2 minutes, until the razor clams pop open and the meat has detached from the side of the shells. Remove the pan from the heat and tip the clams into a colander placed in the sink, covering them with ice to stop the cooking process.

Meanwhile, make the nam jim dipping sauce and set aside.

To prepare the razor clams, remove the cooked meat from the shells and set the shells to one side. Using a sharp knife, remove the gut from the clams (it's the dark brown part in the middle) and discard. Cut the remaining meat into 1-cm/½-in pieces. Mix the clam meat in a bowl with the diced tomatoes, spring onions and passion fruit seeds and 3 tbsp of the nam jim dipping sauce.

Lay out the clam shells on a serving dish and spoon the clam mixture back into the shells. Sprinkle with the coconut, coriander and red amaranth, and serve.

Serves 4

1 kg/2 lb 4 oz razor clams
ice, for cooling
10 cherry tomatoes, finely diced
2 spring onions (scallions), finely sliced
1 tsp passion fruit seeds
½ quantity Nam Jim Dipping Sauce (see p. 26), about 3 tbsp

For the garnish:
2 tbsp grated fresh coconut or desiccated (dried grated) coconut
a small handful of coriander (cilantro), finely chopped, or micro-coriander
a sprinkling of red amaranth micro-herbs, if available (you can source these online or some specialist greengrocers stock them)

Pairs well with
Pinot Gris

Hot Tapas

We've kept the same approach to hot food as we had to the cold food of our earlier years, keeping things simple, but making sure that everything has that punch of flavour. Don't be shy about trying out the recipes with different species of fish or shellfish; there aren't any official rules on what goes with what, so have a bit of fun.

Monkfish Cheeks with Mushroom Broth and Seaweed

Whilst we were renovating our Padstow restaurant, I was lucky enough to be given the opportunity to work in Paul Ainsworth's kitchen at No. 6, just around the corner from our place. It was really eye-opening – the attention to detail, the passion and the organization – I was inspired. One awesome technique I picked up was the use of Marmite, mixed with a little butter, to add richness to the meat that it is brushed on. The most suitable fish I found to use this technique on is monkfish. If you can't find monkfish cheeks, the recipe works just as well with a similar quantity of monkfish fillet.

_____

Preheat the oven to 160°C fan/180°C/350°F/gas mark 4.

Place the dried porcini mushrooms in a bowl, pour over the warm water and set aside.

In a large saucepan, warm a splash of olive oil over a medium heat, add the shallots and garlic and cook for about 10 minutes, until softened.

Add the thyme sprigs and the porcini mushrooms, including their soaking water. Bring to the boil, then lower the heat, add the fresh mushrooms and leave to simmer for 15 minutes.

Place the monkfish on a plate, drizzle with olive oil and season with salt and pepper on both sides.

In a small saucepan, gently melt the butter and mix in the Marmite. Once combined, pour into a warmed ramekin and set aside.

Heat a little olive oil in a griddle or frying pan (skillet) set over a medium-high heat. Add the monkfish and fry for 2 minutes on each side. Transfer the fish to a roasting pan and baste with the buttery Marmite on both sides. Roast in the hot oven for 5 minutes, then remove and allow to rest for 3 minutes.

Ladle the mushroom broth equally into 4 wide serving bowls. Divide the roasted monkfish cheeks between the bowls, and crumble over some dried seaweed, to garnish.

Serves 4

30 g/1 oz dried porcini mushrooms
700 ml/24 fl oz/3 cups warm water
olive oil, for cooking and drizzling
4 shallots, finely sliced
2 garlic cloves, finely chopped
4 thyme sprigs
200 g/7 oz mixed fresh mushrooms, roughly chopped
600 g/1 lb 5 oz monkfish cheeks, cut into 4 or 8 pieces
sea salt and freshly ground black pepper
50 g/1¾ oz/3½ tbsp unsalted butter
1 tsp Marmite (yeast extract)
dried dulse seaweed, to garnish

Pairs well with
Pinot Noir

Thai Crab Cakes with Sweet Chilli Dipping Sauce

We're so lucky to have amazing crab available to us in Padstow (and also in London, as we send it up to the restaurant overnight from the coast). There's nothing better than a whole crab, with some great bread and aioli – but admittedly, it's messy and very labour-intensive. These crab cakes are a great way of eating crab without feeling as though you need a bath after your meal!

To make the sweet chilli sauce, blend the garlic, chillies, sugar, water, vinegar and salt to a rough purée in a food processor. Transfer to a saucepan and bring to the boil. Reduce the heat and simmer for about 3 minutes, until the mixture thickens. Combine the cornflour and water to make a paste and add to the saucepan with the chilli mixture. Bring to the boil and cook for about 1 minute. Leave to cool, then store in the fridge until needed.

Preheat the oven to 160°C fan/180°C/350°F/gas mark 4.

Combine all the crab cake ingredients (except the olive oil) in a large bowl and mix thoroughly. Shape into 8 evenly sized balls, then flatten each slightly between the palms of your hands to make a patty.

Heat a large, ovenproof, non-stick frying pan (skillet) over a medium heat. Add a drizzle of olive oil and fry the crab cakes for 2 minutes on each side, until golden. Be careful not to break them up. Transfer the frying pan to the hot oven for 5 minutes, to cook the cakes all the way through.

Remove from the oven and transfer to a serving plate. Scatter the spring onions over the top and serve with the lime wedges on the side, for squeezing over the top. Serve with the sweet chilli sauce.

Pairs well with
Riesling from Alsace, Australia or New Zealand

Serves 4 (makes 8 cakes)

For the sweet chilli sauce:
3 garlic cloves, peeled
2 medium fresh red chillies, stalks removed, seeds intact
170 g/6 oz/generous ¾ cup caster (superfine) sugar
180 ml/6 fl oz/¾ cup water
60 ml /2 fl oz/4 tbsp white wine vinegar
½ tsp table salt
1 tbsp cornflour (cornstarch)
2 tbsp water

For the crab cakes:
200 g/7 oz white crab meat (unpasteurized)
75 g/2½ oz/1 cup panko breadcrumbs
1 fresh red chilli, finely sliced
4 spring onions (scallions), finely sliced
4 tbsp chopped coriander (cilantro)
2 garlic cloves, finely sliced
2 tsp finely chopped fresh ginger
zest of 1 lime
75 g/2½ oz fine green beans, finely sliced
1 tbsp crème fraîche
1 tbsp Vietnamese Marinade (see p. 24)
1 egg
olive oil, for cooking

For the garnish:
2 spring onions (scallions), finely sliced
1 lime, cut into wedges

Sand Sole
a la Plancha

After our first year of the Padstow restaurant being open, we thought it would be awesome to take the guys from both Islington and Padstow on a staff trip to Barcelona. It was a great chance to spend some time together and gain a bit of inspiration. We had so many great meals, but one that stood out was when we perched at a bar and had all sorts of seafood simply cooked on the plancha (hot plate) with a drizzle of parsley oil. That, combined with some ice-cold white wine, was one hell of a lunch!

Lay the fish out on a tray, drizzle a little oil on both sides and season well with salt and pepper.

Add the extra-virgin olive oil, parsley and garlic to a food processor, blend for 2–3 minutes and set to one side.

Heat a frying pan (skillet), large enough to hold the 2 fish, over a medium heat and add a little olive oil. Lay the fish in the pan and fry for 4–5 minutes. Flip the fish over and cook for a further 4–5 minutes. If you are using lemon sole, or any other chunky flat fish, you may need to additionally roast the fish in the oven for a few minutes at 160°C fan/180°C/350°F/gas mark 4, to cook through.

Once cooked, transfer to a serving dish and generously drizzle the parsley oil over the fish. Squeeze over fresh lemon, to taste.

Serves 4

2 x 250–300 g/9–10½ oz sand sole, skinned (alternatively use Dover sole, lemon sole or megrim)
olive oil, for drizzling
sea salt and freshly ground black pepper
100 ml/3½ fl oz/7 tbsp good-quality extra-virgin olive oil
a small bunch of parsley, roughly chopped
1 garlic clove, peeled
lemon wedges, to serve

Pairs well with
Albariño

Cod with Feta, Wild Garlic and Pine Nuts

Cheese and fish are ingredients that you wouldn't immediately associate with each other. However, feta, with its salty-sour flavour, works fantastically well when combined with the fresh herbs and wild garlic. We pick our wild garlic from a shaded walled area close to the beach in Padstow, and near to my grandparents' house in London. It's only in season for a couple of months from March onwards.

Preheat the oven to 160°C fan/ 180°C/350°F/gas mark 4.

Heat an ovenproof frying pan (skillet) over a medium-high heat. Add the butter. Score the skin of the cod fillets, drizzle with a little of the olive oil and season. Place the fillets in the pan, skin-side down, and fry for 2–3 minutes to crisp up the skin. Turn the fillets over and fry for another minute.

Transfer the frying pan to the hot oven and roast the fish for 8 minutes.

Meanwhile, combine the remaining olive oil, feta, wild garlic, basil, mint, dill, lemon juice, pine nuts and white wine vinegar in a bowl. Season well and mix thoroughly.

Remove the frying pan from the oven, transfer the fish to a serving dish, and pour the cheese dressing over the fish to serve.

Serves 4

1 tsp unsalted butter
4 x 200 g/7 oz cod fillets, skin on
100 ml/3½ fl oz/7 tbsp good-quality extra-virgin olive oil
sea salt and freshly ground black pepper
100 g/3½ oz feta cheese, crumbled
a small bunch of wild garlic, leaves roughly chopped (keep some of the flowers if you can, for garnish)
a small bunch of basil, roughly chopped
a small bunch of mint, roughly chopped
a small bunch of dill, roughly chopped
juice of ½ lemon
2 tsp pine nuts, toasted
a splash of white wine vinegar

Pairs well with
Sancerre
Pouilly-Fumé

This is one of the most popular dishes at POTL. 'Nduja is a spicy sausagemeat from Calabria, in southern Italy. We buy ours from a small producer who makes it in Dorset. The recipe works amazingly well with squid. We cross-score the flesh, which allows the squid to cook more quickly, as well as allowing the flavours to penetrate the meat further.

Heat a saucepan over a medium heat and add the 'nduja, butter and lemon juice. Heat until the butter has melted, then thoroughly mix the ingredients together in the pan. You can keep this mixture, refrigerated, for up to a week – you will need to mix it intermittently as it cools and sets. It can be reheated in the pan when needed.

Place the squid pieces in a bowl and pour over half of the melted 'nduja mixture. Mix well, ensuring the squid is covered thoroughly in the 'nduja butter.

Heat a large, non-stick frying pan (skillet) over a high heat and drizzle in a little olive oil. Place the squid tentacles in the pan first, as they take a little longer to cook and don't be tempted to move the squid. After a minute or so, add the scored body and wings, placing the scored side down. The scored pieces will curl up; when this happens, turn the tentacles over along with the wings and scored body, and cook for a further 2 minutes.

Place the squid in a serving dish. Pour over any cooking juices left in the pan, as well as the remaining 'nduja butter, and garnish with the tarragon leaves. Serve immediately.

Serves 4

125 g/4½ oz 'nduja sausagemeat
125 g/4½ oz/½ cup unsalted butter
juice of ½ lemon
4 medium squid, cleaned, body scored and cut into pieces, tentacles and wings included
olive oil, for frying
3 sprigs of tarragon, leaves only

Squid with 'Nduja and Tarragon

Pairs well with
Verdejo

Roasted Scallops with Vietnamese Marinade and Peanuts

This dish utilizes the shells of the scallops. It's simple to prepare, but great for showing-off to mates (or the in-laws!). If possible, source hand-dived scallops – although they are more expensive, they have little impact on the ocean and aren't treated with any preservatives or chemicals, as dredged scallops can be. You could replace the scallops with oysters; simply shuck the oysters and follow the same process.

Preheat the oven to 160°C fan/180°C/350°F/gas mark 4.

Arrange the scallops in their shells in a roasting pan. Mix the Vietnamese marinade and the coconut milk together and spoon this equally over the scallops. Sprinkle half the sliced spring onion over the scallops and roast in the hot oven for 12 minutes.

Once cooked, transfer the scallops in their shells onto a serving dish. We sit the shells on a bed of seaweed, but if this isn't available then some finely sliced baby gem (Boston) lettuce leaves could be used to hold the shells in place. Sprinkle the toasted peanuts over, followed by the remaining spring onion, and garnish with the coriander leaves.

Serves 4

4 scallops, in the half shell
4 tbsp Vietnamese Marinade (see p. 24)
2 tbsp coconut milk
2 spring onions (scallions), finely sliced
a small handful of toasted peanuts, crushed
8 coriander (cilantro) leaves

Pairs well with
A fruity German Riesling
New Zealand Sauvignon
Torrontés

Tempura Pollock with Curry Sauce and Crispy Capers

Serves 4

Pollock has always been known as a cheaper alternative to cod – it is not quite as flakey, but I do love the flavour. This recipe is great for any white fish: plaice, haddock or whiting. You can't go wrong when you tempura fish.

To make the curry sauce, set a saucepan over a medium heat, drizzle in a little olive oil, add the shallots, chillies and garlic, and cook until softened. Set aside.

In a separate dry frying pan (skillet), set over a medium heat, toast the coriander, cumin and fennel seeds and cardamom pods for about 1 minute. Transfer to a spice grinder or pestle and mortar and grind to a powder.

Put the saucepan with the softened shallots, chillies and garlic back over a low heat and add the ground spices. Add in the cinnamon and turmeric and mix thoroughly. Add in the chopped tomatoes and coconut milk and simmer for 15 minutes. Remove from the heat and blend the mixture to a sauce. Pass the sauce through a sieve to remove any bits. If the sauce is too runny, you can return it to the heat for a few minutes, to reduce.

In a small frying pan (skillet) set over a medium heat, add a little olive oil and fry the capers for a couple of minutes, until crispy. Remove to some paper towels and pat dry. Set aside.

For the batter, combine the dry ingredients in a mixing bowl and mix thoroughly. Slowly add the chilled sparkling water, whisking thoroughly until you achieve the consistency of double (heavy) cream.

Ideally, use a deep-fat fryer (if you haven't got one, use a heavy-based saucepan) and heat the vegetable oil to 190°C/375°F. Test the temperature with a kitchen thermometer or when a cube of bread dropped in the oil sizzles immediately.

Coat the pollock strips in the batter mix and fry in batches for about 1 minute, until they are just about to turn golden. Remove with a slotted spoon and transfer to some paper towels to absorb any excess oil, and season.

Pour the curry sauce into a serving dish, pile the tempura on top, and garnish with the crispy capers, spring onion, coriander leaves and lime wedges.

For the curry sauce:
olive oil, for frying
2 shallots, finely sliced
2 bird's eye chillies, finely chopped
4 garlic cloves
2 tsp each of coriander seeds, cumin seeds and fennel seeds
1 tsp black cardamom pods
1 tsp ground cinnamon
2 tsp ground turmeric
1 x 400 g/14 oz can of chopped tomatoes
1 x 400 ml/14 fl oz can of coconut milk

For the crispy capers:
olive oil, for frying
3 tbsp capers

For the tempura batter:
75 g/2½ oz/½ cup plain (all-purpose) flour
50 g/1¾ oz/½ cup cornflour (cornstarch)
1½ tsp baking powder
approx. 150 ml/5 fl oz/scant ⅔ cup chilled sparkling water

vegetable oil, for frying
400 g/14 oz pollock, skinned and cut into thin strips
sea salt and freshly ground black pepper
2 spring onions (scallions), finely sliced, to garnish
a few coriander (cilantro) leaves, to garnish
lime wedges, to garnish

Steamed Mussels and Cockles in a Coconut and Lemongrass Broth

Our Vietnamese marinade packs a real flavour punch on its own, but when you combine it with the juices released from the shellfish it creates a tasty broth. Grab some crusty bread to mop up all those juices. You could also use palourde clams, razor clams and/or even throw some prawns (shrimp) in when steaming, to add an extra element to the recipe.

Choose to purchase live mussels and cockles. The mussels should have securely closed shells. If they are open, tap them on a hard surface; if they close they are still alive and fine to eat. The shells of the mussels should be damp and shiny, although this is less noticeable with cockles. Avoid mussels and cockles with broken, cracked or split shells – discard these before cooking.

Mix the Vietnamese marinade and coconut milk together in bowl.

Heat a large, lidded saucepan over a high heat. Once hot, add the mussels and cockles, pour the coconut milk mix over the molluscs and cover with the lid. Cook for about 3–4 minutes, shaking from time to time, until all the molluscs have popped open. Discard any that have remained closed.

Divide between 4 bowls, with an equal amount of broth in each, or transfer to one large serving dish. Garnish with the chopped spring onions, mint and coriander leaves and serve with wedges of lime. Some soda bread or a crusty loaf is also great to have to hand, for dunking in that broth.

Serves 4

6 tbsp Vietnamese Marinade (see p. 24)
200 ml/7 fl oz/scant 1 cup coconut milk
1 kg/2 lb 4 oz live mussels
600 g/1 lb 5 oz live cockles

For the garnish:
4 spring onions (scallions), chopped
a small handful of mint leaves
a handful of coriander (cilantro), roughly torn
4 lime wedges

soda bread (see p. 156) or crusty bread, to serve

Pairs well with
Albariño

Prawn and Oyster Mushroom Noodle Soup

A quick and easy dish; your mates will think you've spent years living in the Vietnamese countryside mastering the art of a mega-tasty, warming soup!

Heat a saucepan over a medium heat, add the coconut oil and red onion and cook for a few minutes to soften. Add the mushrooms and, once these have softened a little, add the Vietnamese marinade and stir in thoroughly. Add the stock, coconut milk and boiling water.

Bring up to the boil, then add the noodles. Reduce to a simmer and cook for 3 minutes.

Finally, add the prawns and the pak choi. If using raw prawns, cook until they have changed from a grey colour to pink; if cooked, just allow a minute for the prawns to heat through.

Transfer to individual bowls, or one large serving bowl, and scatter the garnishes over the soup, to serve.

Pairs well with
New Zealand
Pinot Noir

Serves 4

2 tsp coconut oil or olive oil
2 red onions, finely sliced
100 g/3½ oz oyster mushrooms (or a mixture of different mushrooms), roughly chopped
8 tbsp Vietnamese Marinade (see p. 24)
350 ml/12 fl oz/1½ cups fish or vegetable stock
250 ml/9 fl oz/1 generous cup coconut milk
500 ml/17 fl oz/2 generous cups just-boiled water
150 g/5½ oz fresh wholewheat noodles
16 tiger prawns (shrimp), raw or cooked, head and shell on or off, whatever you prefer
2 small or 1 large pak choi (bok choy), quartered

To garnish:
4 spring onions (scallions), finely sliced
1 fresh red chilli, deseeded and sliced
a small handful of coriander (cilantro), chopped
a small handful of mint, chopped

North African Spiced Mackerel

Martin Murt is one of the local fishermen we work with and when he brings mackerel into our Padstow restaurant, this dish goes straight on the menu. It's hugely popular as mackerel is actually caught just outside Padstow, so you really can't get much fresher.

Preheat the oven to 160°C fan/ 180°C/350°F/gas mark 4. Alternatively, bring a barbecue up to temperature.

Using a sharp knife, score the mackerel along both sides of the body and season with a little salt.

Heat a heavy-based frying pan (skillet) over a medium heat and toast the coriander and cumin seeds until fragrant (about 1 minute), then transfer to a spice grinder or pestle and mortar and crush. Add the crushed spices to a food processor, along with the garlic, paprika, preserved lemon, a splash of the lemon-preserving liquor, parsley, chopped coriander, tomato purée and olive oil, and blend for 1 minute.

Line a roasting pan with some greaseproof (wax) paper and place the mackerel on top. Rub the spice paste over the mackerel and into the scored flesh.

Roast in the hot oven for 8 minutes. Alternatively, cook over the hot barbecue for about 4 minutes on each side.

Transfer the fish to a serving plate, and garnish with the reserved coriander leaves and lime wedges.

Serves 4

4 mackerel, gutted and cleaned
sea salt
1 tbsp coriander seeds
1 tbsp cumin seeds
4 garlic cloves, peeled
2 tbsp paprika
1 preserved lemon, plus a splash of the liquor from the jar
1 small bunch of parsley, roughly chopped
1 small bunch of coriander (cilantro), roughly chopped, with a few leaves reserved for garnish
1 tsp tomato purée (tomato paste)
40 ml/1¼ fl oz/2½ tbsp olive oil
lime wedges, to serve

Pairs well with
A fresh, cold lager
A light wheat beer
A spicy red wine, such as Rioja

S + MUSSELS FROM THE
HE ESTUARY IN PORTHILLY, ROCK
SHARP'S
CORNISH
Pilsner

Our supplier, Johnny Murt, often has rockling come up in his crab and lobster pots. It's almost unheard of to see it in a restaurant or fishmongers, but I find it suits a tempura batter perfectly – the meat is soft and this marries beautifully with the crunch of the batter. If you can't get hold of rockling, this recipe works just as well for cheaper fillets of fish, such as plaice, coley or whiting.

Mix the plain flour, cornflour and baking powder together, then slowly add the chilled sparkling water, whisking as you go. You're aiming for the consistency of double (heavy) cream and you may need to use less or more water than the quantity listed.

Heat the vegetable oil in a pan or wok deep enough to submerge the strips of fish. You can test when it has reached 190°C/375°F with a kitchen thermometer or when a cube of bread dropped into the oil sizzles immediately. Alternatively use a deep-fat fryer.

Dust the strips of fish in a little flour, then coat them in the batter mix and carefully lower into the hot oil. You may need to do this in 2 batches. Once golden, remove with a slotted spoon and drain on paper towels.

Transfer to a serving plate. Sprinkle with the sliced chilli, mint and spring onions and serve immediately, with the nam jim dipping sauce on the side.

Serves 4

75 g/2½ oz/½ cup plain (all-purpose) flour, plus a little for dusting
50 g/1¾ oz/½ cup cornflour (cornstarch)
2 tsp baking powder
approx. 150 ml/5 fl oz/scant ⅔ cup chilled sparkling water (you may need more or less)
vegetable oil, for frying
300 g/10½ oz rockling or other white fish, skinned and cut into thin strips
1 fresh red chilli, thinly sliced
a small handful of mint leaves
2 spring onions (scallions), finely sliced
100 ml/3½ fl oz/7 tbsp Nam Jim Dipping Sauce (see p. 26), to serve

Rockling Tempura with Nam Jim

Pairs well with
Sharps Cornish Pilsner Lager

Octopus with Coriander Butter Beans and Mojo Verde

Octopus isn't the easiest thing to cook, but following this recipe should ensure a melt-in-the-mouth texture. Combine this with the punch of flavour from the spicy coriander beans and you've got a match made in heaven!

Heat a splash of olive oil in a pot large enough to hold the octopus, over a low-medium heat. Add the garlic and soften for a minute, then add the bay leaves and the octopus and cover with a lid. Cook for 30 minutes. After this time, top up with boiling water, ensuring the octopus is completely covered. Cook for a further 1 hour, then remove the octopus and allow to cool.

In a separate saucepan, heat another splash of olive oil over a medium heat and add the shallots, garlic and chilli. Sweat until softened, then add the butter beans, white wine and stock and keep on a low simmer for 20 minutes to reduce slightly.

In a spice grinder or pestle and mortar, add a small bunch of coriander with a drizzle of olive oil and grind to a paste. Add this mixture to the butter beans and stir thoroughly. Season to taste.

To make the mojo verde, add all the ingredients to a food processor and blend for 2 minutes to a fine paste.

Once cool, cut the head off the octopus and discard, then separate the individual tentacles. Drizzle a little olive oil over the tentacles and season well.

Heat a large, non-stick frying pan (skillet) over a medium heat. Add a little oil to the pan, then add the tentacles, cooking for about 1 minute on each side.

To serve, spoon some of the butter beans onto each plate, top with the tentacles, then spoon the mojo verde over the tentacles. Garnish with the reserved coriander leaves.

Pairs well with
A dry, crisp, lemony white wine, such as Albariño

Serves 4

olive oil
3 garlic cloves, crushed
2 bay leaves
1 x 2 kg/4 lb 8 oz Mediterranean octopus, cleaned (frozen Mediterranean octopuses are usually already cleaned. Avoid English octopuses – they are too difficult to cook)

For the butter (lima) beans:
olive oil
3 banana shallots, finely sliced
6 garlic cloves
1 green bird's eye chilli, finely sliced
800 g/1 lb 12 oz canned butter (lima) beans, drained
100 ml/3½ fl oz/7 tbsp white wine
250 ml/9 fl oz/1 generous cup chicken stock
a small bunch of coriander (cilantro), a few leaves reserved to garnish
sea salt and freshly ground black pepper

For the mojo verde:
a small bunch of coriander (cilantro), blanched for a few seconds in boiling water
2 garlic cloves
juice of ½ a lime
½ tsp cumin seeds
75 ml/2¼ fl oz/4½ tbsp extra-virgin olive oil
generous pinch of sea salt

We are so lucky to have Porthilly oysters growing in the estuary a stone's throw from the restaurant in Padstow. Tim and Luke Marshall care so much about their product. During the busy times of the season we sometimes run out – one call to the guys and they shoot over in their boat and drop them off – legends! In the restaurant, we garnish these with micro-fennel. It's difficult to get, but if you want to go the extra mile, it's worth it.

Shuck the oysters, removing the meat into a sieve to drain any excess liquid (this will keep the oysters crispy and you can use the juice to make a Dirty Oyster Martini, see p. 172). Keep the cupped (not the flat) part of the shells, and arrange on a serving plate. You can use a stack of rock salt to steady the shells, or some seaweed if you can get hold of it.

Ideally, use a deep-fat fryer and heat the oil to 190°C/375°F. You can also use a deep, heavy-bottomed pan or wok, but take care with the hot oil.

Coat the oysters in the flour and fry in the hot oil for 2 minutes. Remove with a slotted spoon onto paper towels to drain.

To serve, add a teaspoon of garlic crème fraîche into each oyster shell. Place a deep-fried oyster on top of the crème fraîche and garnish with a sliver of spring onion and some micro-fennel, if you have it.

Serves 4

12 meaty and plump oysters (Porthilly, if possible)
vegetable oil, for frying
plain (all-purpose) flour, for dredging
1 quantity Garlic Crème Fraîche (see p. 27)
2 spring onions (scallions), sliced into thin slivers and kept in ice-cold water until ready to serve, for garnish
micro-fennel, for garnish (optional)

Deep-fried Porthilly Oysters with Garlic Crème Fraîche

Pairs well with
Sparkling Albariño
Prosecco

Smoked Haddock Scotch Egg with Romesco Sauce

Pairs well with
Pinot Noir
Lager

Everyone loves Scotch eggs; well, proper ones, not those supermarket mass-produced dry things, but the ones you cut open to reveal a runny yolk. One of only a few labour-intensive recipes in this book, it's all in the preparation. These can be made a day or so in advance, and are bound to impress.

For the romesco sauce, preheat the oven to 160°C fan/180°C/350°F/gas mark 4.

Spread the almonds and bread over a baking tray (cookie sheet) and place in the oven for 8–10 minutes, to toast the nuts and dry the bread out. Remove and allow to cool.

Add the almonds, bread and all the remaining sauce ingredients to a food processor and blend until smooth. You may need to add some extra olive oil. Set aside.

For the Scotch eggs, bring a saucepan of water to the boil and carefully drop the 4 whole eggs in. Boil for 6 minutes, then remove immediately into iced water to stop the cooking process.

Add the parsley and smoked haddock to a food processor and blend to a paste. Remove and divide the mixture into 4 portions. Roll each into a ball, then flatten out on a non-stick surface (greaseproof (wax) paper works well). If your mixture breaks up, add a little olive oil to moisten.

Remove all the shells from the soft-boiled eggs and place each onto a circle of haddock paste. Carefully wrap the eggs in the paste, completely covering them.

Prepare 3 dishes: one filled with flour, one with beaten egg and the last with breadcrumbs. First, roll the wrapped eggs in flour to cover, then roll in the beaten egg, then finally roll in the breadcrumbs, ensuring they are all completely covered.

In a deep saucepan, add a depth of 8 cm/3¼ inches of vegetable oil and heat over a high heat to 190°C/375°F. Add the breadcrumbed eggs and cook for around 5 minutes. You will need to gently turn the eggs to ensure they are nice and golden all over. You could also do this in a deep-fat fryer, if you have one.

Spoon the romesco sauce onto a serving dish and place the Scotch eggs on top. Alternatively, serve the sauce on the side.

Serves 4

For the romesco sauce:
80 g/2¾ oz/1 cup flaked (slivered) almonds
1 slice of stale white bread
100 g/3½ oz roasted red (bell) peppers
2 garlic cloves
1 tsp paprika
1 tbsp sherry vinegar
3 tbsp extra-virgin olive oil

For the Scotch eggs:
5 large free-range hen's eggs: 4 whole, 1 beaten
iced water, for cooling
a handful of parsley
400 g/14 oz undyed smoked haddock, skin removed
plain (all-purpose) flour, for dusting
100 g/3½ oz/scant 1 cup panko breadcrumbs
vegetable oil, for frying

Butterflied Sardines with Mango Salsa

Sardines are such an awesome species to cook – so quick, cheap, tasty and sustainable. Make sure they are as fresh as possible.

The mango salsa transports me straight back to sitting round the table with my parents and brothers. Mum used to make this when she served fajitas and, coupled with the oiliness of the sardines, it's bang on!

Place the sardines on a baking tray (oven pan), skin-side up, drizzle with olive oil and season.

Mix the mango, red onion, chilli, coriander and lime juice together with a drizzle of olive oil. Set aside.

Heat a drizzle of olive oil in a non-stick frying pan over a medium-high heat. Place the butterflied sardines into the pan, skin-side down. The meat of the fish will gradually change colour from a pinkish red to an opaque white. When it gets halfway up the side of the fish, flip the sardines over and cook for a further 30 seconds.

You can also cook these on a barbecue. Once it is up to temperature, oil the rungs of the barbecue with olive oil, then oil and season the skin of the fish and follow the same method as for cooking in a pan.

Transfer to a serving plate, spoon on a pile of the mango salsa and garnish with the coriander leaves.

Serves 4

12 sardines, butterflied (ask your fishmonger to do this)
olive oil, for drizzling
sea salt and freshly ground black pepper
½ mango, peeled, stoned and cubed
½ small red onion, finely diced
1 fresh red chilli, deseeded and finely sliced
a small bunch of coriander (cilantro), roughly chopped, with some leaves reserved for garnish
juice of 1 lime

Pairs well with
Vinho Verde

Crispy Falmouth Bay Shrimp with Sriracha Crème Fraîche

We don't have any large native prawns around the shores of the UK, so we have to import ours from further afield. Many people aren't even aware that we do have this fantastic species of British shrimp; although not very large, they are super-tasty. When deep-fried you can eat the whole thing, head and all. Any good fishmonger should be able to source these for you in season from late summer to early autumn, with some notice. Please give them a go!

This recipe needs to be cooked and served immediately, so have everything ready to go.

Ideally, use a deep-fat fryer (if you haven't got one, use a heavy-based saucepan) and heat the vegetable oil to 180–190°C/350–375°F.

Add the shrimp to a mixing bowl, sprinkle with seasoned flour, and turn with your hands, ensuring the shrimp are completely coated. Transfer to a sieve to remove any excess flour.

Now, carefully pour the shrimp into the hot oil and fry for 2–3 minutes, until crispy. Remove with a slotted spoon and place on paper towels to absorb any excess oil.

Transfer to a serving dish and sprinkle with a little sea salt. Mix the crème fraîche and sriracha together and serve on the side as a dipping sauce, along with lemon wedges to squeeze over the shrimp.

Serves 4

vegetable oil, for frying
200 g/7 oz Falmouth Bay/Mylor shrimp (small shrimp)
plain (all-purpose) flour, seasoned with sea salt and freshly ground black pepper, for dredging
sea salt, to taste
4 tbsp crème fraîche
1 tbsp sriracha chilli sauce
lemon wedges, to serve

Pairs well with
A Cornish white wine, such as Knightor Trevannion

Corn on the Cob and Brown Shrimp with Bone Marrow and Anchovy Butter

It's such a great time of year when corn on the cob is in season. It's available all year round these days, but for the best quality and flavour, buy British-grown corn in the summer months. Using bone marrow sounds complicated, but it's super simple and adds an extra richness to the dish.

Preheat the oven to 160°C fan/ 180°C/350°F/gas mark 4.

Place the marrow bone on a roasting pan and cook in the hot oven for about 10 minutes. Remove from the oven and set aside to cool slightly.

Once the marrow bone is cool enough to handle, scoop out the marrow and add to a food processor, along with the butter, anchovy fillets and a generous drizzle of the oil reserved from the anchovy can. Blend the mixture

until smooth. Using a plastic spatula, scrape the butter from the food processor into a bowl, cover with cling film (plastic wrap) and store in the fridge until needed.

Bring a large pan of lightly salted water to a gentle simmer. Make sure the pan is large enough to fit the corn in. Add the corn cobs and simmer for about 5 minutes.

Meanwhile, add half of the bone marrow and anchovy butter to a small pan set over a medium heat. When the butter has melted, add the shrimp and fry for 2–3 minutes.

Drain the corn and transfer to a serving dish. Pour over the shrimp and butter mixture, and sprinkle with a little smoked paprika. Serve with the remaining butter in a dish on the side, for anyone who likes extra buttery corn!

Serves 4

For the bone marrow and anchovy butter:
1 beef marrow bone, split lengthways
100 g/3½ oz/7 tbsp unsalted butter, at room temperature
2 salted anchovy fillets (reserve some of the oil from the can)

4 corn cobs, husk removed if necessary
90 g/3¼ oz peeled brown shrimp (miniature shrimp)
pinch of smoked paprika

Pairs well with
Vinho Verde

Before I found my love of cooking, I spent 6 months living in China. There, I experienced some incredible food, unlike any other food I'd ever eaten. The use of Szechuan pepper, with its slightly numbing effect, is one of the distinctive flavours that etched itself upon my mind. Making a batch of this salt flavouring gives you a great little store cupboard secret weapon. It can be used on chips, deep-fried potatoes, crispy squid or when searing tuna.

To make the Szechuan salt, heat a frying pan (skillet) over a medium heat and toast the Szechuan pepper and black peppercorns for about 1 minute, to release their aroma. Transfer to a spice grinder and blitz thoroughly. Alternatively, crush as finely as possible in a pestle and mortar. Finally, combine with the Chinese five spice in a non-reactive (glass, ceramic or stainless steel) bowl and set aside.

Add the table salt to the frying pan, increase the heat to high, and cook for about 2–3 minutes, stirring occasionally, until the salt turns slightly grey (although a colour change is not essential). Tip the hot salt into the bowl with the rest of the spices and mix, to fuse the flavours together. Set aside and allow to cool. Kept in an airtight container, this salt will keep for about 6 months.

Bring the frying pan back up to a medium heat and drizzle in a little olive oil. Place the prawns in the pan, drizzle a little more olive over them and generously sprinkle about 2–3 tbsp of the flavoured salt over the prawns. Cook for about 2 minutes, until the prawns have changed from their natural grey colour to pink on the underside, then flip them over, sprinkle with a little more Szechuan salt and cook for a further 2 minutes. Transfer to a serving platter and garnish with the limes.

Serves 4

For the Szechuan salt:
1 tbsp Szechuan pepper
2 tbsp black peppercorns
4 tbsp Chinese five spice
9 tbsp table salt

For the prawns:
olive oil, for frying
12 raw tiger prawns (jumbo shrimp)
2 limes, halved

Szechuan Prawns

Pairs well with
Lager
Merlot

Stuffed Mussels with Capers, Garlic and Parsley

I'm not going to lie, this is a slightly labour-intensive recipe, but it's one that can be done well in advance of mates coming over and the mussels are very quick to cook. It's such a great way to eat these tasty molluscs.

Heat a large saucepan over a medium heat. Add the mussels, with a splash of water, and cover with a tight-fitting lid. Steam for about 3–4 minutes, until the mussels pop open. Tip into a colander, discarding any that have remained closed, and allow to cool.

Put the bread into a food processor and blend into fine crumbs. Add the butter, garlic, lemon zest and juice, Parmesan, parsley, capers and the white wine vinegar to the crumbs and blend again, until everything is well mixed.

Break off one half of the mussel shell from each mollusc and cover the meat of the mussel with a teaspoon of the stuffing mixture. Place them all on a baking tray (oven pan). If not cooking immediately, cover with cling film (plastic wrap) and store in the fridge.

When ready to cook, heat the grill (broiler) to high and, placing the tray quite close to the grill, grill (broil) the stuffed mussels for 2–3 minutes, until the mixture has turned a golden brown and the butter has melted. Transfer to a serving platter and get stuck in!

Serves 4

36 large live mussels, beards removed
2 thick slices of day-old bread, torn into pieces
150 g/5½ oz/⅔ cup unsalted butter
6 garlic cloves, roughly chopped
zest of 1 lemon and the juice of ½
2 tbsp grated Parmesan cheese
a medium bunch of parsley, roughly chopped
a small handful of capers, roughly chopped
a splash of white wine vinegar

Pairs well with
A lemony white wine, such as Albariño

Pan-fried Whole Squid with Capers, Preserved Lemon and Tarragon

Keeping squid whole and frying in the pan gives you a great contrast in textures — the wings crisp up and the body should melt in your mouth. Combine this with the dressing in this recipe and you'll find it's a match made in heaven! When buying your squid, ask your fishmonger to keep the wings of the squid attached — these parts are usually thrown away, but when pan-fried have a great flavour.

Mix together all the dressing ingredients and set aside.

Lay the squid out, so the wings are flat on the board. Using a sharp knife, carefully score the top side of the squid, ensuring these scores don't go through to the underside of the hood. Pat the squid and tentacles dry with paper towels, drizzle with olive oil and sprinkle with a little salt.

Heat a frying pan (skillet), large enough to hold all the squid, until nice and hot. Add the tentacles first as these need a little more cooking than the body. After 1 minute, lay the body in the pan with the wings flat on the surface of the pan. Don't be tempted to move the squid, just let it cook for about 2 minutes, until it has built up some golden colour, then flip it over and repeat.

Place the squid on the serving plates and spoon over the dressing, having given it a good mix beforehand. Add another sprinkle of salt and serve, with lemon wedges on the side.

Serves 4

For the dressing:
1 tbsp capers, chopped
2 tbsp white balsamic or sherry vinegar
a small handful of tarragon, chopped
1 tbsp preserved lemon, chopped
2 tsp of liquor from the preserved lemon jar
3 tbsp extra-virgin olive oil
1 garlic clove, finely chopped
1 banana shallot, finely chopped

4 squid, cleaned and kept whole, including tentacles, around 800 g/1lb 12 oz in total
extra-virgin olive oil, for drizzling
sea salt, to taste
wedges of lemon, to serve

Pairs well with
A dry, pale and crisp rosé from Provence or the Loire Valley

Crab-stuffed Courgette Flowers

This recipe combines the produce from two of our best suppliers. Ross has a kitchen garden just outside Padstow, and grows incredible veg; Johnny fishes crab and lobster for us just out of the Camel Estuary. Both have been a huge support to us, as well as becoming good friends. Understated in appearance (the dish, not Ross and Johnny!), it takes just one bite and you'll not want to share!

In a mixing bowl, add the crab meat, crème fraîche, spring onions and lemon juice and mix together, seasoning to taste.

Gently open the petals of the courgette flowers and spoon equal amounts of the crab mixture in between the petals, packing the mix in tightly and leaving enough space to be able to twist the petals back together. Ensure there are no gaps for the crab to escape out of.

Ideally, use a deep-fat fryer (if you haven't got one, use a heavy-based saucepan) and heat the vegetable oil to 190°C/375°F. Test the temperature by putting a cube of bread in the oil – if it immediately starts to crisp up, you're ready to go.

Meanwhile, make the tempura batter. Mix the plain flour, cornflour and baking powder together and slowly add the chilled sparkling water, whisking as you go. You're aiming for the consistency of double cream (you may need to add more or less than the quantity given – be guided by the consistency).

Gently coat the stuffed flowers in the batter and, using a spoon for support, slowly lower a flower into the hot oil, flower-end first. After a few seconds, let it submerge fully and fry for about 1½ minutes, until golden. Repeat for all 4 flowers.

Remove with a slotted spoon and place on paper towels to absorb any excess oil. Season with sea salt and they're ready to serve.

Serves 4

150 g/5½ oz white crab meat (unpasteurized)
1 tbsp crème fraîche
2 spring onions (scallions), finely sliced
1 tsp lemon juice
sea salt and freshly ground black pepper
4 courgette (zucchini) flowers, with the baby courgettes still attached
1 litre/35 fl oz/4⅓ cups vegetable oil

For the tempura batter:
75 g/2½ oz/½ cup plain (all-purpose) flour
50 g/1¾ oz/½ cup cornflour (cornstarch)
1½ tsp baking powder
approx. 150 ml/5 fl oz/scant ⅔ cup chilled sparkling water (you may need more or less)

Pairs well with
Chablis
Chardonnay

Whole Crispy Red Mullet with Lemon and Olive Oil

I had this very dish on the Greek island of Corfu, sat at plastic tables and chairs, looking across the bay with Katie and my parents. We all agreed that this dish was something special, both in flavour and simplicity. Whenever I eat it, I'm transported back to that trip.

A deep-fat fryer is the best thing to use for this recipe. If you don't have one, heat vegetable oil in a frying pan (skillet) large enough to fit the 4 fish. The oil needs to be deep enough to submerge half of the fish when laid on their sides. Bring the oil up to 190°C/375°F. Test the temperature by putting a cube of bread in the oil – if it immediately starts to crisp up, you're ready to go.

Pat the fish dry with paper towels, then dust with flour, ensuring they are completely covered and any excess is shaken off. Carefully place the fish in the hot oil. Fry for 4 minutes on each side. Remove with a slotted spoon onto some paper towels to absorb any excess oil.

Transfer to a serving plate, sprinkle with sea salt and serve with lemon wedges and the dressing in a small bowl on the side.

Serves 4

vegetable oil, for frying
4 red mullet, around 300 g/
    10½ oz each, scaled and gutted
    (gurnard can be used as an
    alternative)
plain (all-purpose) flour, for dusting
sea salt, to taste
lemon wedges, to serve
approx. 3–4 tbsp Extra-virgin Olive
    Oil and Lemon Dressing (see p. 25)

Pairs well with
English, Greek or
Italian lager
A dry crisp rosé
wine

Palourde Clams with Manzanilla and Garlic

Combining good-quality sherry with the amazing liquor from steamed clams creates an awesome, tasty sauce to mop up with some fresh crusty bread. The aroma will send you wild!

In a medium saucepan, set over a medium heat, add a little olive oil and cook the garlic and shallots until softened. Add the clams to the pan, along with a generous glug of Manzanilla sherry. Cover the pan with a lid and cook for about 1–2 minutes, until the clams open. Discard any that have not opened. Transfer to a serving dish and garnish with the parsley. Serve with some crusty bread on the side.

Serves 4

extra-virgin olive oil, for cooking
4 garlic cloves, finely chopped
2 banana shallots, finely chopped
1.2 kg/2 lb 12 oz live palourde/surf clams
a generous glug of Manzanilla sherry
finely chopped parsley, to garnish

Pairs well with
A crisp white wine, such as Muscadet

Cooking this recipe gets the senses going – the moment it goes into the oven, it fills the room with an fantastic aroma and you can't wait to tuck in! Once you've mastered the curry marinade, you can use it for other fish, such as fillets of cod or salmon, or whole fish such as bass or bream.

For the curry marinade, heat the butter in a frying pan (skillet) over a medium heat, add the onion, garlic and chilli and fry for about 5 minutes, until softened.

Meanwhile, heat a separate dry frying pan over a medium heat and toast the cumin and coriander seeds and cloves for about 1 minute to release the aromas. Transfer to a spice grinder, or pestle and mortar, and grind to a powder.

Add the softened onion, garlic and chilli to a food processor, along with the ground spice mix, cinnamon, lemon juice and coriander. Add a pinch of sea salt and the olive oil, then blend for about 1 minute to a rough, textured paste.

Preheat the oven to 160°C fan/180°C/350°F/gas mark 4.

Roughly score the mackerel on both sides to allow the curry marinade to penetrate the flesh of the fish. Line a roasting pan with some greaseproof (wax) paper and drizzle over a little oil to stop the mackerel sticking. Place the mackerel onto the paper and spoon the curry marinade over the mackerel, evenly coating the fish on both sides.

Roast the fish in the hot oven for 10–12 minutes.

Transfer to a serving dish and scatter with the toasted peanuts and sliced spring onion.

Serves 4

For the coriander curry:
1 tbsp salted butter
1 small white onion, roughly chopped
2 garlic cloves, finely chopped
1 fresh bird's eye chilli, finely sliced
½ tsp cumin seeds
½ tsp coriander seeds
¼ tsp whole cloves
¼ tsp ground cinnamon
juice of ½ lemon
1 medium bunch of coriander (cilantro)
pinch of sea salt
3 tbsp extra virgin olive oil

4 mackerel, gutted and cleaned (ask your fishmonger to do this for you)
2 tbsp crushed toasted peanuts, to serve
3 spring onions (scallions), finely sliced, to serve

Mackerel and Coriander Curry with Toasted Peanuts

Pairs well with
Riesling
Grüner Veltliner
IPA

Large Plates

There's nothing better than having one big dish to put down in the middle of the table for everyone to tuck into. For the perfect group meal, mix up some of the small tapas plates to start off with, then finish off with a showstopper from this section.

Salt-baked Sea Bream

Salt baking fish is the ultimate recipe for a bit of dining theatre, as well as a great way of keeping the fish moist. You can experiment with different dry herbs to mix in with the salt to adjust the flavour.

Preheat the oven to 180°C fan/ 200°C/400°F/gas mark 6.

In a large mixing bowl, mix the salt, eggs and fennel seeds together to form a paste.

On a roasting pan, spread out half the salt mixture across the tray. Lay the fish on top, then stuff the cavity of the fish with half of the lemon wedges and all of the rosemary and thyme. Cover the fish with the remaining salt, ensuring the whole fish is completely covered, and pat

it down smoothly. Cook in the hot oven for 15 minutes.

Remove from the oven and leave the fish to rest for 5–10 minutes – this will allow the fish to continue cooking gently. After this time, give the salt crust a good bash with a rolling pin or the back of a knife. Use a large spoon to remove the chunks of salt, then carefully peel off the skin of the fish, trying not to let the salt touch the flesh.

You may want to serve the fish straight from the roasting pan, as it looks quite dramatic. Alternatively you can carefully transfer to a serving dish. Be sure to remove the skin, as it will be covered in salt. Serve with the remaining lemon wedges and a green salad.

Serves 4

2 kg/4 lb 8 oz coarse sea salt
4 free-range eggs
4 tsp fennel seeds
1 x 1.25 kg/2 lb 12 oz or 2 x 600 g/ 1 lb 5 oz sea bream (wild if available), scales on but gutted
2 lemons, cut into wedges
1 large bunch of rosemary
1 large bunch of thyme

Pairs well with
Picpoul de Pinet

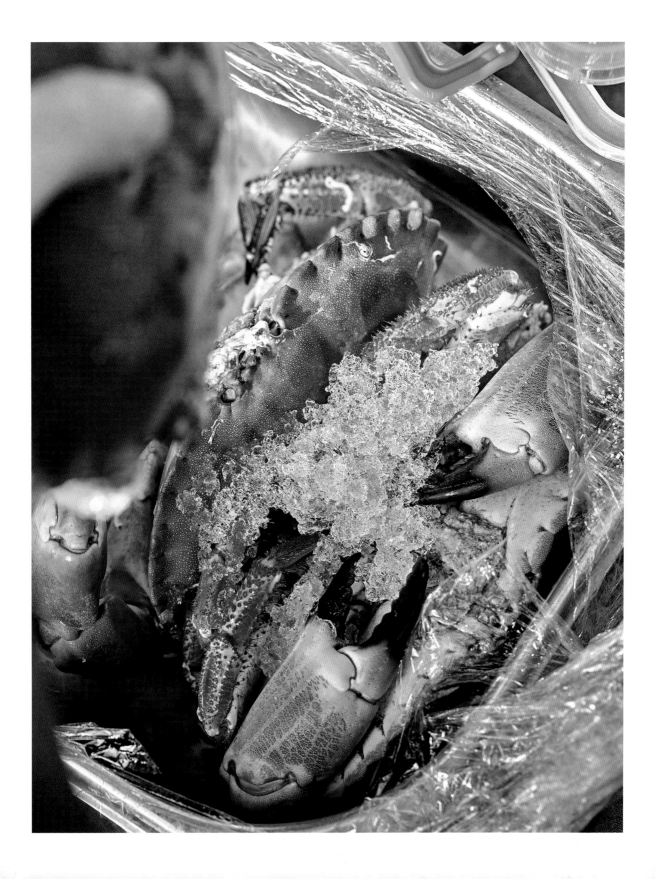

Roast Turbot with Mediterranean Vegetables and Salsa Verde

Pairs well with
A full-flavoured dry white wine, such as Meursault

Turbot is undeniably one of the tastiest fish around. It has to be cooked whole – the reason being that so much flavour comes from the bones. Roasting it on top of vegetables allows all the tasty juices from the fish to be soaked up by what's beneath. This is definitely a recipe for a special occasion, as turbot is one of the more expensive species, but it will impress.

Preheat the oven to 140°C fan/ 160°C/325°F/gas mark 3.
In a large roasting pan put the courgette, pepper, red onion, tomatoes and the unpeeled garlic cloves, drizzle with plenty of olive oil, and season well. Spread half the rosemary over the vegetables, add a splash of red wine vinegar and roast in the hot oven for 25 minutes.

Meanwhile, lay the fish out on a board and, using a sharp knife, score it down the middle, then make about 4 scores on each side, fanning outwards. Drizzle with olive oil, then tuck the peeled, sliced garlic into the scores along with the remaining rosemary. Season the fish and lay the lemon slices on top.

After they have roasted for 25 minutes, remove the vegetables from the oven. Turn the oven heat up to 160°C fan/180°C/350°F/gas mark 4. Place the fish on top of the vegetables and return to the oven to roast for a further 35 minutes.

Meanwhile, place all the ingredients for the salsa verde into a food processor and pulse until roughly blended.

Remove the fish from the oven, drizzle over the salsa verde and serve straight from the roasting dish. You could serve some nice crusty bread on the side to mop up the juices, or crushed spiced potatoes (see p. 150).

Serves 4

1 courgette (zucchini), roughly chopped
1 red (bell) pepper, roughly chopped
3 red onions, quartered
150 g/5½ oz cherry tomatoes, halved
8 garlic cloves, unpeeled, plus 4 garlic cloves, peeled and finely sliced
good-quality extra-virgin olive oil, for drizzling
sea salt and freshly ground black pepper
1 bunch of rosemary, leaves only
a splash of red wine vinegar
1.25–1.5 kg/2 lb 12 oz–3 lb 5 oz turbot, fins trimmed
1 lemon, sliced into rounds

For the salsa verde:
a small handful of basil
a small handful of mint
a small handful of flat-leaf parsley
1 garlic clove, peeled
4 anchovy fillets
2 tbsp capers
2 tsp red wine vinegar
6 tbsp good-quality olive oil

Covering a whole fish with this marinade is a sure-fire way of getting loads of flavour into any fish. It's not too overpowering and brings an awesome fresh, clean taste that you often don't get when eating out. This method works equally well on flat and round fish. Although not essential, when using flat fish, ask your fishmonger to remove the top layer of skin for you, to ensure the marinade flavours penetrate the meat. If the skin is still present, or if using round fish, just score the skin before marinating.

Preheat the oven to 160°C fan/ 180°C/350°F/gas mark 4. Line a roasting pan, large enough to hold the monkfish tail, with greaseproof (wax) paper.

Spread 2 tablespoons of the marinade across the greaseproof paper and place the monkfish tail on top. Make sure the meat of the butterflied monkfish is opened out and spread the remaining marinade over the fish. If you are using a different fish you may need more or less marinade – just make sure the fish is well covered.

Sprinkle with half the spring onion and roast in the hot oven for 20 minutes. When the fish is cooked, the meat will start to peel away from the backbone.

Transfer to a serving plate and pour the cooking juices over the fish. Garnish with the remaining spring onion, coriander, basil and peanuts (if using). Serve with lime wedges on the side.

Serves 4

8 tbsp Vietnamese Marinade (see p. 24)
1.5 kg/3 lb 5 oz monkfish tail on the bone, skinned and butterflied (ask your fishmonger to do this)
4 spring onions (scallions), finely sliced
4 sprigs of coriander (cilantro), leaves only
4 sprigs of holy basil (Thai basil), leaves only
a handful of toasted peanuts, chopped (optional)
1 lime, cut into wedges

Whole Roasted Monkfish Tail with Vietnamese Marinade

Pairs well with
Pinot Gris
Riesling

Johnny Murt's Crab Adobo

When we first started coming to Padstow to visit Johnny Murt, one of our suppliers who quickly became a great friend, he cooked up his signature dish of Chicken Adobo for us. Although renowned in the town, I wasn't so sure, looking at the amount of soy and cider vinegar going into the pot. However, when we came to eat it, I was amazed! Given that Johnny is a crab fisherman, I suggested we tried it with whole crab next time, and it worked so well. You can either use whole crab and pour the sauce over, or use crab claws, mixing it all in together. Make sure you serve a nice fresh salad with it (Johnny is a salad dodger!).

Heat a small saucepan over a medium heat, add a drizzle of olive oil, then add the garlic and ginger, cooking for about 2–3 minutes, until softened. Add the soy sauce, cider vinegar and bay leaves and leave to simmer for 15 minutes.

Meanwhile, preheat the oven to 160°C fan/180°C/350°F/gas mark 4.

Arrange the crab claws on a roasting pan and put them in the oven to warm through. This should only take 4–5 minutes.

Carefully transfer the crab claws into a serving dish, as the shells will be hot. Pour over the hot adobo dressing and garnish with the spring onions, the mooli or radish matchsticks and plenty of lime wedges.

Serves 4

olive oil, for drizzling
5 garlic cloves, finely sliced
4 tsp finely chopped fresh ginger
100 ml/3½ fl oz/7 tbsp soy sauce
100 ml/3½ fl oz/7 tbsp cider vinegar
2 bay leaves
8 large crab claws
4 spring onions (scallions), sliced
100 g/3½ oz mooli (daikon), peeled and sliced into matchsticks, or sliced radishes
lime wedges, to serve

Pairs well with
Pinot Gris
Riesling
Lager

BBQ Carabineros Prawns with Olive Oil and Sea Salt

Barbecuing these Mediterranean prawns is a brilliant way of adding a smoky element to these sweet-flavoured beauties. If you can't barbecue them, you can always grill or fry them. Sucking the prawn heads is mandatory! It's one of the easiest recipes ever, but the prawns have such a beautiful natural flavour, they really don't need much adding to them.

When your barbecue is up to temperature, drizzle the prawns with olive oil and season generously with sea salt. Lay the prawns on the barbecue, along with the lemon halves, and grill for 2 minutes, then flip the prawns over and grill for another 2 minutes. Check that the lemon halves are nicely charred.

Transfer to a serving plate and drizzle a little extra-virgin olive oil over them and season with salt and pepper. Garnish with the charred lemon.

Serves 4

12 raw carabineros prawns (jumbo shrimp)
olive oil, for grilling
2 lemons, halved
good-quality extra-virgin olive oil, for drizzling
sea salt and freshly ground black pepper

Pairs well with
Fino sherry
Cava

For the last few years, I've been lucky enough to be involved in a trip to Italy organized by our wine supplier, Tim. In a Tuscan hill-top town called Panzano, I had the ultimate meat experience... At Antica Macelleria Cecchini, where meat is life, the whole meal was amazing, but I just couldn't stop eating the whipped lardo! Added to whole roasted fish, it brings an amazing richness to the flavour.

For the truffled lardo, add the lardo, garlic, herbs and sea salt to a food processor and blend. Slowly pour in the truffle oil and keep blending until a light paste forms. You may have to remove the lid and push the lardo back into the bowl of the processor. If the lardo has not formed a light paste, add a little olive oil to loosen.

Preheat the oven to 160°C fan/180°C/350°F/gas mark 4. Line an oven tray, large enough to fit the fish and onions alongside each other, with greaseproof (wax) paper.

Score the skin on top of the brill, drizzle with olive oil and tuck the garlic slices into the scores. Drizzle olive oil over the red onions, splash with a little white wine vinegar and season well. Cover the fish with foil and roast in the hot oven for 30–40 minutes. Remove the foil 5 minutes before the end of this cooking time and spoon over the whipped lardo. Leave the fish uncovered for these final 5 minutes.

Transfer to a serving dish or serve straight from the roasting pan.

Serves 4

For the whipped truffled lardo:
150 g/5½ oz lardo (cured pork fat), skin removed and diced
1 garlic clove, peeled
1 tsp dried rosemary
1 tbsp dried thyme
a generous pinch of sea salt
1½ tbsp white truffle oil
olive oil (optional)

1.5 kg/3 lb 5 oz whole brill, fins trimmed (if you're feeling extravagant, turbot could also be used)
good-quality extra-virgin olive oil (Italian, if possible)
3 garlic cloves, finely sliced
4 small red onions, halved
a few splashes of white wine vinegar
sea salt and freshly ground black pepper

Whole Brill with Truffled Lardo and Red Onions

Pairs well with
Mâcon-Villages
A rich white Burgundy, such as Chablis

My first job when I moved to London was working front of house at a well-known seafood restaurant, previously owned by Mitch Tonks. The stand-out dish, and one that has stayed with me ever since, was the seafood stew. Sadly for me, Mitch was no longer involved in the restaurant when I worked there, so I never had the chance to learn it directly from him. This is my version of his recipe. I've cooked this many times for friends and family and it's such a sociable dish that gets everyone diving in.

In a food processor, combine all the parsley oil ingredients, blend well, and set aside.

For the stew, heat the olive oil in an extra-large lidded saucepan set over a low heat. Add the shallots, chilli, garlic and thyme, and sweat for about 2–3 minutes, until soft. Add the Pernod and cook for a further 3 minutes to cook off the alcohol. Add the fennel and cook for about 5 minutes, until soft. Add the tomatoes and saffron and cook for another 10 minutes.

Add the wine and fish stock. (If you want to add any steaks of fish, such as ray, bass, bream or gurnard, you could add them at this point.) Cook for 4 minutes, then add all the shellfish and cover with a lid to allow it to steam.

Once the mussels and clams have popped open, about 4–5 minutes, drizzle with the parsley oil and chopped basil and bring the pot to the table to serve. Some crusty bread is a must.

Serves 4

For the parsley oil:
100 ml/3½ fl oz/7 tbsp olive oil
1 garlic clove
3 sprigs of flat-leaf parsley

For the stew:
8 tbsp olive oil
2 shallots, finely chopped
1 fresh red chilli
4 garlic cloves, finely chopped
10 thyme sprigs, leaves only
1 fennel bulb, chopped
6 medium-sized tomatoes, quartered and roasted (roasting is optional)
2 pinches of saffron
a generous splash of Pernod
200 ml/7 fl oz/scant 1 cup white wine
150 ml/5 fl oz/scant ⅔ cup fish stock
600 g/1 lb 5 oz live mussels
350 g/12 oz live clams
4 langoustines
4 raw tiger prawns (jumbo shrimp), heads and shell on
a small handful of basil leaves, chopped, to garnish

Shellfish Stew with Parsley Oil

Pairs well with
Muscadet
Albariño

Whole Crab with Lime and Coriander Butter

This dish can be prepared in the oven, but it's also a great dish to do on the barbecue. We typically use this butter with crab and lobster, but you could also use it with crab claws, langoustines, or skinned flat fish such as Dover sole. The lime really cuts through the heaviness of the butter. It's a lovely social dish for everyone to tuck into.

Ask your fishmonger to remove the 'dead man's fingers' from the crabs and to split the bodies in half and crack the claws for you.

Preheat the oven to 160°C fan/ 180°C/350°F/gas mark 4, or get your barbecue up to temperature.

Place the crabs on a baking tray (oven pan) and put them into the hot oven. Cook for about 5 minutes, without turning. Alternatively, cook on the barbecue (not on the hottest part, or the shells will burn), turning halfway through, for 3–4 minutes on each side, until cooked through.

In the meantime put the butter, lime juice and salt and pepper into a small saucepan. Over a low heat, stir the butter constantly with a whisk, until the butter and lime juice have completely emulsified, leaving you with a smooth and silky sauce.

The crabs should be ready by the time the sauce is finished. Remove the crabs from the oven or barbecue (careful – they'll be hot!) and stack them up on a serving platter.

Throw most of the chopped coriander into the sauce (reserving a little for garnish), give it a good stir, then pour over the crabs. Scatter over the reserved coriander and spring onions, if using, and garnish with the lime halves.

Serves 4

2 cooked crabs, about 1 kg/
   2 lb 4 oz each
125 g/4½ oz/generous ½ cup
   unsalted butter, cubed
juice of 1 lime
pinch of sea salt and freshly ground
   black pepper
a small handful of chopped
   coriander (cilantro)
2 spring onions (scallions), finely
   sliced (optional)
1 lime, halved

Pairs well with
Pinot Gris
Gavi

Lobster with Smoked Chorizo Butter

Using chorizo is an amazing way of getting a slightly meaty, smoky flavour into the fish or shellfish you're cooking with. As with the previous recipe, it's great on crab and lobster, but you can also experiment with other species of fish. This lobster is perfect when served with the Tomato and Tarragon Salad (see p. 154) and/or our Crushed Spiced Potatoes (see p. 150). You can get smoked butter from delis or online.

Heat a saucepan or frying pan (skillet) over a medium heat and add a drizzle of olive oil. Add the chorizo and fry gently for 3–4 minutes, until it releases its oils.

Meanwhile, preheat the oven to 160°C fan/180°C/350°F/gas mark 4, or get your barbecue up to temperature.

Place the split lobster body and claws on a baking tray (oven pan) and put into the hot oven for 5 minutes. Alternatively cook on the barbecue (not on the hottest part, or the shells will burn), turning halfway through, for about 2 minutes on each side, basting with olive oil.

By now, the chorizo should have softened nicely, so add the smoked butter, lemon juice and seasoning, reduce the heat to low, and stir until the butter has melted.

Take the lobsters out of the oven/ off the barbecue (careful – they'll be hot!), place on a serving dish and pour the chorizo butter over the lobster. Sprinkle over the chopped chives and serve.

Serves 4

a drizzle of olive oil
100 g/3½ oz cooking chorizo, finely diced
2 cooked lobsters, split in half and claws cracked
125 g/4½ oz/generous ½ cup smoked butter
juice of ½ lemon
pinch of sea salt and freshly ground black pepper
a small bunch of chives, roughly chopped

Pairs well with
Sancerre
A white Burgundy such as Chablis

Monkfish and Chorizo Stew

Monkfish is one of those fish that can convert any non-fish eater. With dense flesh and no awkward little bones to pick through, it suits a pairing with meat very well. This is an awesome dish to chuck in the middle of the table and let everyone delve in.

Heat a large saucepan over a medium heat and add a good drizzle of olive oil. Add the chopped rosemary, fennel, red onions, garlic and chorizo and cook until softened, around 10 minutes.

Add the red wine and cook for a further 10 minutes. Add the tomato purée, chopped tomatoes, smoked paprika and the Marmite, check the seasoning, and mix well. Reduce the heat slightly and simmer gently for 45 minutes.

The chorizo stew can be made a couple of days before you need to use it, as long as it is kept in the fridge. If you've done this, heat it up in a saucepan before you use it in the dish, as the fish will not cook evenly if it's cold.

Preheat the oven to 160°C fan/ 180°C/350°F/gas mark 4.

In a large roasting pan spread out the hot chorizo stew. Lay the monkfish over the top of the stew, adding another drizzle of olive oil and seasoning with salt and pepper. Spike the reserved rosemary sprigs into the fish and cook in the hot oven for 25–30 minutes.

To finish, garnish with some fresh tarragon leaves and another little drizzle of olive oil. Serve with roasted potatoes or thick crusty bread.

Serves 4–6

olive oil, for drizzling
a handful of rosemary, finely chopped, plus 4 sprigs reserved whole
1 fennel bulb, finely sliced
2 red onions, finely diced
10 garlic cloves, finely chopped
200 g/7 oz good-quality cooking chorizo, finely diced
300 ml/10½ fl oz/generous 1¼ cups red wine
1 tbsp tomato purée (tomato paste)
3 x 400 g/14 oz cans of good-quality chopped tomatoes
2 tsp smoked paprika
2 tsp Marmite (yeast extract)
sea salt and freshly ground black pepper
1.5 kg/3 lb 5 oz monkfish tail on the bone, skinned and butterflied (ask your fishmonger to do this)
tarragon leaves, to garnish

Pairs well with
Red Rioja (slightly chilled)

Roasted Ray Wing with Olives, Chilli and Agridulce

Chef Mitch Tonks and our wine supplier Tim introduced me to agridulce vinegar, an amazing ingredient that turns a simple dish into something very special. Ray (skate) wings are one of my favourite fish – the meat slides off the top of the cartilage in long strands and has a wonderful texture and flavour.

Preheat the oven to 160°C fan/ 180°C/350°F/gas mark 4.

Line a roasting pan with a sheet of greaseproof (wax) paper. Drizzle with a little of the olive oil and place the ray wing(s) on top.

In a mixing bowl, combine the remaining ingredients and mix thoroughly. This can be done in advance and kept in the fridge. If you do this, make sure you remove the mixture from the fridge 30 minutes before using, to allow it to come back to room temperature.

Spoon the mixture evenly over the wing(s) and roast in the hot oven for 20 minutes. The cooking time will be a little less if you are using smaller wings, as they will be much thinner. Here's a great trick that our head chef Rob taught me, to check if the wing is cooked: using a pair of tongs, gently twist the piece of bone at the thickest point of the wing. If it disconnects easily from the flesh, it's time to remove the wing from the oven.

Once cooked, transfer carefully to a serving dish and pour the cooking liquor over the wing(s). Sprinkle over a little sea salt and serve.

Serves 4

3 tbsp extra-virgin olive oil

1.5 kg/3 lb 5 oz ray (skate) wing (can be 1 large or several smaller wings)

150 g/5½ oz mixed pitted olives, finely sliced

1 fresh red chilli, split in half lengthways and finely sliced

2 garlic cloves, finely chopped

2 tbsp agridulce vinegar (alternatively use a sweeter white wine vinegar)

sea salt, to taste

Pairs well with
Alsace Pinot Gris

I lived in China for 6 months in my days after university. Struggling to get a job in design, I finally got a placement ... on the other side of the world! One weekend, a colleague took me fishing near her home town. We took the fish to a roadside restaurant and they made us a dish similar to this – well, as close as I could match it anyway!

Ideally you want to buy a grey mullet that has been caught at sea, rather than an estuary-caught mullet, which can have a stronger earthy taste – ask your fishmonger.

Preheat the oven to 160°C fan/ 180°C/350°F/gas mark 4. Line a roasting pan with greaseproof (wax) paper.

Score both sides of the mullet's skin, about 1 cm/½ in apart, to allow the flavour to enter the fish. Place the fish on the lined dish and rub the garlic into the scores.

Mix the soy sauce and mirin together and pour over the fish, then sprinkle the Chinese five spice over. Cover with the strips of carrot, spring onion and sliced chilli and add a final drizzle of olive oil all over the fish. Cook in the hot oven for 20 minutes.

To finish, sprinkle over a little more Chinese five spice, and garnish with chilli and spring onion.

Serves 4

1.5 kg/3 lb 5 oz grey mullet, scaled and gutted (ask your fishmonger to do this)
2 garlic cloves, finely sliced
2 tbsp dark soy sauce
2 tbsp mirin
1 tbsp Chinese five spice
2 carrots, peeled and sliced into thin strips
2 spring onions (scallions), sliced into thin strips
1 fresh red chilli, sliced
olive oil, for drizzling

For the garnish:
1 tsp Chinese five spice
1 fresh red chilli, finely sliced
2 spring onions (scallions), sliced into thin strips

Chinese-style Grey Mullet

Pairs well with
Gamay
Grüner Veltliner

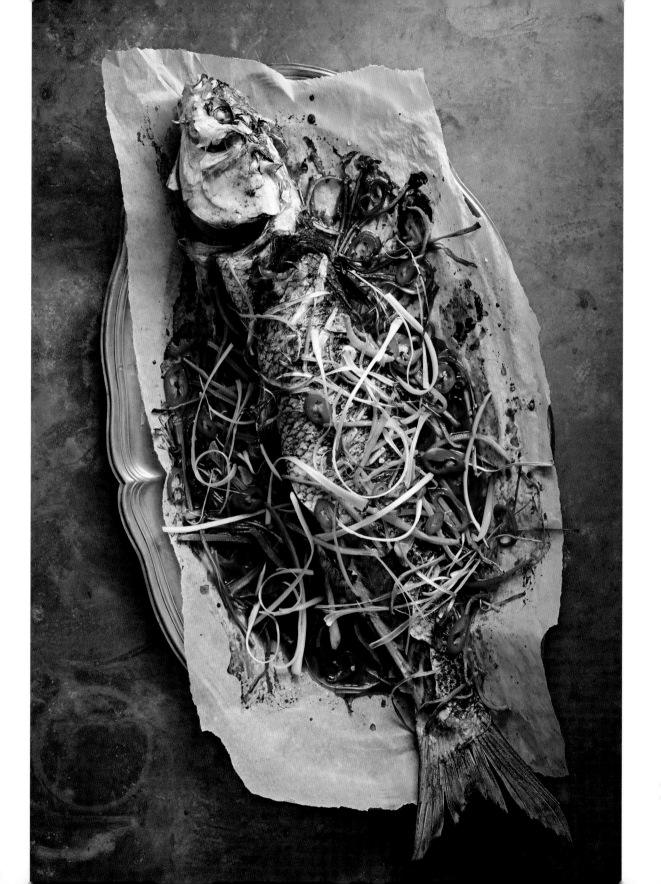

Sides

Side dishes should never be an after-thought and are just as important as the main event. They don't need to be labour-intensive or time-consuming; by combining just a few different ingredients you can create something that really complements the seafood you are serving. Here, we've put together our favourite sides from the last few years.

Brown Shrimp with Asparagus, Pak Choi and Cashews

The brown shrimp in this recipe are optional, so the dish could be used as a veggie dish or as a side to accompany other fragrant dishes. We use Cornish asparagus from Ross and from St Enodoc, across the estuary from Padstow. It's only a short season, so when asparagus is available, we make the most it.

In a large saucepan, bring some lightly salted water to the boil, add the asparagus and cook for 30 seconds. Drain the asparagus, then immediately plunge into iced water. Pat dry with paper towels.

Combine the cooked asparagus, cucumber, pak choi, radishes, brown shrimp and nam jim dipping sauce in a mixing bowl and toss together thoroughly. Transfer to a serving plate, sprinkle the cashews and coriander over the top and garnish with the lime halves. Add sea salt, to taste.

If you prefer, you can switch the brown shrimp for prawns (shrimp), crab or even poached squid.

Serves 4

1 bunch of asparagus, woody stalks removed, sliced in half if large
iced water, for cooling
½ a cucumber, cut into ribbons with a peeler or a mandolin
1 pak choi (bok choy), cut into strips
6 radishes, finely sliced
100 g/3½ oz brown shrimp (miniature shrimp)
4 tbsp Nam Jim Dipping Sauce (see p. 26)
a small handful of toasted cashew nuts, crushed
a small handful of coriander (cilantro), chopped
2 limes, halved
sea salt

Pairs well with
Riesling

Crushed Spiced Potatoes

Rick doesn't like chips (controversial, we know!), but our customers were constantly asking for them. So, after playing around, this is what we came up with – a boiled potato/chip hybrid, that is more addictive than Pringles! We fry the potatoes for a crispy crunch – if you oven roast them, they won't be crunchy, although they will still be delicious.

This recipe makes a large quantity of spiced salt, but you can keep it in an airtight jar and use it whenever you like – it will keep for about 6 months.

In a large saucepan, add the potatoes, cover with cold water and bring to the boil. Parboil the potatoes for about 15 minutes, until soft, then drain and set aside.

Meanwhile, make the spiced salt. Heat a heavy-based frying pan (skillet) over a high heat and toast the cumin, coriander and fennel seeds for about 1 minute, until aromatic. Add them to a spice grinder and blitz, or crush in a pestle and mortar, then combine in a non-plastic mixing bowl with the other powdered spices.

Set the frying pan back over a high heat, add the salt and heat for about 2–3 minutes, until the salt turns a grey colour (although a colour change is not essential). Add to the mixing bowl and carefully combine the hot salt with the other spices (this helps the flavours of the spices to infuse the salt). Set aside to cool.

Gently crush the cooked potatoes on a board, under the palm of your hand, or use a potato masher to press them.

If you have a deep-fat fryer, heat the oil to 190°C/375°F. Fry the potatoes, in batches if necessary, for about 4–5 minutes, until golden. Drain on paper towels.

Otherwise, preheat the oven to 160°C fan/180°C/350°F/gas mark 4. Place the crushed potatoes in a large bowl and drizzle with olive oil, turning them to coat thoroughly. Spread the potatoes over a roasting pan and cook in the oven for 25–30 minutes, turning them every so often, until crispy and golden. Remove from the oven.

Sprinkle about 1–2 tsp of the spiced salt over the fried or roasted potatoes, giving them a good shake to ensure all the potatoes are well covered.

Place in a serving bowl and garnish with the chopped coriander and spring onion.

Serves 4

500 g/1 lb 2 oz new potatoes

For the spiced salt:
1 tsp cumin seeds
1 tsp coriander seeds
1 tsp fennel seeds
1 tsp smoked paprika (pimentón)
2 tsp ground turmeric
½ tsp ground cinnamon
100 g/3½ oz/⅓ cup table salt

vegetable oil, for deep-frying, or a drizzle of olive oil, for oven baking
a small handful of coriander (cilantro), chopped, to garnish
2 spring onions (scallions), thinly sliced, to garnish

Baby Gem Lettuce with Truffle Oil and Grana Padano

This side dish is super simple and mega tasty. The key is to use a good-quality truffle oil – it's really worth spending a little more to enhance this dish to its best.
If you can't find Grana Padano, you can substitute Parmesan.

Simply fan out the baby gem leaves on a serving dish or platter to enable the oil and cheese to reach all of the leaves. Drizzle the truffle oil all over, then sprinkle with the grated cheese. If you are really truffle-obsessive, you can drizzle a little more oil over the cheese. Grind black pepper over the top and serve immediately.

Serves 4

2 baby gem (Boston) lettuces, leaves
   separated, washed and dried
white truffle oil, for drizzling
4 tbsp shaved Grana Padano cheese
freshly ground black pepper

Tim, our good friend and wine supplier, introduced us to an amazing balsámico that is made close to Barcelona in Spain. This light and sweet vinegar takes this salad to another level. If you can't find the Ferret Guasch Balsámico that we use, any light sweet balsamic or sweetish sherry vinegar will work too. Make sure you buy tomatoes that are nice and ripe, preferably still on the vine.

In a mixing bowl, combine all the ingredients and mix thoroughly. Then simply transfer to a serving dish. Another option would be to arrange the salad leaves on a platter and spoon the tomato mixture over to serve.

Serves 4

350 g/12 oz vine-ripened tomatoes, roughly chopped
2 garlic cloves, finely chopped
3 sprigs of tarragon, leaves only, roughly chopped
3 tbsp good-quality extra-virgin olive oil
3 tbsp light, sweet balsamic vinegar
freshly ground black pepper
a generous pinch of sea salt
mixed salad leaves, to serve (optional)

Tomato and Tarragon Salad

Pattie's Soda Bread

I'm lucky enough to have two dads! Before we started Prawn on the Lawn, we'd come home to a house smelling of my stepdad Pattie's freshly baked soda bread. It's an awesome bread, as there's no proving needed, so from start to finish you can make it in just under an hour.

Preheat the oven to 160°C fan/ 180°C/350°F/gas mark 4. Grease a 900 g/2 lb loaf tin (pan) and dust lightly with a little flour.

Put the plain flour, wholemeal flour, bicarbonate of soda and salt into a large bowl and combine thoroughly. Add the buttermilk and mix with your hands until a dough forms. It's important to mix the dough as little as possible, to ensure a good rise.

Transfer the dough to the loaf tin and bake in the hot oven for 45 minutes, until golden. Remove from the oven, turn it out from the tin and leave to cool on a wire rack.

Serves 4

a little butter or oil for greasing the tin
115 g/4 oz/scant 1 cup plain (all-purpose) flour, plus a little for dusting the tin
340 g/11¾ oz/2¾ cups wholemeal (wholewheat) flour
1 tsp bicarbonate of soda (baking soda)
½ tsp table salt
450 ml/16 fl oz/2 cups buttermilk

Poppy Seed and Seaweed Flatbread

This is a fantastic accompaniment to the Whipped Cod's Roe (p. 54), Mackerel Pâté (p. 51) and Cured Salmon (p. 67) recipes. You can experiment with different dry toppings here, if you wish.

Preheat the oven to 160°C fan/ 180°C/350°F/gas mark 4.

Combine the plain and wholemeal flours with the milk in a mixing bowl and knead to a sticky dough. Using a rolling pin, roll out the dough on some greaseproof (wax) paper to a 2–3 mm/⅛ in thickness. Place the dough, on its paper, onto a baking sheet.

Brush the surface of the dough with the egg yolk, and sprinkle over the poppy seeds, seaweed and a pinch of salt.

Bake in the preheated oven for 6–7 minutes. Keep a close eye on it – you want a nice golden colour. Remove from the oven, leave to cool on the baking sheet, and snap into whatever size you want, to serve.

Serves 4

100 g/3½ oz/¾ cup plain (all-purpose) flour
100 g/3½ oz/¾ cup wholemeal (wholewheat) flour
3 tbsp milk
1 egg yolk, whisked
2 tsp poppy seeds
2 tsp dried dulse seaweed
a pinch of salt

You wouldn't expect to find Padrón peppers in Padstow, but Ross Geach at the Padstow Kitchen Garden does a great job at growing them! As soon as these small green peppers come into season, we get them straight on the menu and they go down a storm. Beware though – it's said that 1 in 10 are super hot!!

In a frying pan (skillet) large enough to hold the peppers, heat the olive oil over a medium heat, until smoking hot. Very carefully add the Padrón peppers. Fry, keeping them moving in the pan. As soon as you see the skins start to blister, remove the peppers from the pan with a slotted spoon on to some paper towels. Transfer to a serving dish and sprinkle generously with sea salt flakes, to serve.

Serves 4

3 tbsp extra-virgin olive oil
24 Padrón peppers
sea salt flakes

Fried Padrón Peppers

With this dish, it's all about the ingredients! Asparagus has a very short season (around 6 weeks in the UK), so you really need to make the most of it while you can. We are lucky to have two fantastic suppliers within a couple of miles of the restaurant, so we get it super fresh: St Enodoc Asparagus and Padstow Kitchen Garden. This recipe deviates slightly from the English classic, but the addition of soy sauce really is a game changer and doesn't overpower the flavour of the asparagus.

Remove the woody base of the asparagus by either snapping or cutting it off. When you bend the asparagus, it tends to snap where the woody base meets the tender part of the stem.

To make the soy butter combine the butter, lemon juice and soy sauce in a small saucepan set over a low heat. Stir continuously until melted, then set aside.

Heat a large non-stick frying pan (skillet) over a medium heat. Drizzle the asparagus with olive oil, season with salt, then place into the pan and cover with a lid. Steam for 2 minutes, then turn the asparagus over, replace the lid and cook for a further 2 minutes.

If you need to, reheat the butter slightly. Transfer the cooked asparagus to a serving dish and either pour the butter over the top or serve the butter in a ramekin or small bowl on the side, for dipping.

Serves 4

a large bunch of asparagus, approx. 400 g/14 oz
100 g/3½ oz/7 tbsp unsalted butter
juice of ½ small lemon
1½ tbsp soy sauce
olive oil, for drizzling
sea salt, to season

Charred Asparagus with Soy Butter

Desserts
and Cocktails

Prawn on the Lawn is all about the seafood, so desserts were somewhat of an afterthought in the restaurant, only making it onto the menu after protests from customers to have something sweet to finish! We just keep things simple and only offer a couple, along with a plate of local cheeses and homemade chutney.

Life wouldn't be the same without a dessert to finish your meal off. This one is dangerous!

_____

Melt the butter in a saucepan set over a medium heat. Add the sugar, the double cream, the vanilla and salt, and mix thoroughly. Bring the mixture to the boil, then reduce to a simmer for about 5 minutes, until it thickens slightly.

Place 4 amaretti biscuits into 4 small pots or ramekins (about 240ml/ 8 fl oz/1 cup capacity), and crush lightly with the end of a rolling pin. Carefully pour the hot caramel mixture over the biscuits and transfer to the fridge until needed.

When ready to serve, spoon a little crème fraîche into each pot, top with fresh raspberries and garnish with a sprig of mint.

Serves 4 (or 6 slightly smaller servings)

For the caramel:
125 g/4½ oz/generous ½ cup unsalted butter
210 g/7½ oz/generous 1 cup soft light brown (light muscovado) sugar
150 ml/5 fl oz/scant ⅔ cup double (heavy) cream
¼ tsp vanilla bean paste
2 pinches of sea salt flakes

To serve:
16 amaretti biscuits (cookies) (make sure they're the hard ones, not soft)
350 ml/12 fl oz/1½ cups crème fraîche
200 g/7 oz fresh raspberries (about 12 in total)
4 sprigs of mint

Salted Caramel Pot

Pairs well with
Monbazillac
Sauternes

Lemon Posset and Coconut Shortbread

This is a really simple, fruity and light dessert, ideal for those who say they don't like desserts. You can make the posset and the shortbread a day in advance, so it's really easy to put together at the last minute.

First make the possets. Place a saucepan over a low heat, add the cream and sugar and stir gently, until the sugar has melted. Bring to a simmer and let it bubble away for 1 minute. Take the pan off the heat and stir in the lemon zest and juice. Pour an equal amount into 4 small Kilner jars or ramekins and leave to cool to room temperature. Once cooled, carefully cover with a lid or cling film (plastic wrap) and chill in the fridge for at least 3 hours and up to 24 hours.

Next make the shortbread. Preheat the oven to 160°C fan/180°C/350°F/ gas mark 4.

Spread the coconut out on a small baking sheet and place in the hot oven for about 5–10 minutes, until lightly toasted. Make sure you keep a close eye on it, as it can burn fairly quickly. Set aside to cool.

Line 2 large baking sheets with greaseproof (wax) paper.

Cream the butter and sugar together in a large bowl, using an electric or hand whisk, until light and fluffy. Sift in the flour and cornflour and add the toasted coconut. Mix to form a dough, then roll out to about 1 cm/½ in thick on a lightly floured surface. Use a biscuit cutter to cut out small biscuits and keep re-rolling and cutting until you have used all the dough. Place the biscuits onto the lined baking sheets and sprinkle with some extra coconut. Place in the fridge for about 30 minutes, to stop the shortbread spreading when cooking.

Bake the biscuits in the hot oven for 20 minutes, or until lightly golden. Remove from the oven and leave to cool on the baking sheets for 10 minutes, then transfer to a wire rack to cool completely.

Serve the lemon possets straight from the fridge and place the biscuits on a large plate in the middle of the table so that everyone can help themselves. Store any leftover biscuits in an airtight container – they are great with a cup of tea or coffee.

Serves 4

For the possets:
400 ml/14 fl oz/1¾ cups double (heavy) cream
135 g/4¾ oz/⅔ cup golden caster (superfine) sugar
zest of 2 lemons, plus 50 ml/ 1½ fl oz/3 tbsp juice

For the coconut shortbread:
50 g/1¾ oz/generous ½ cup desiccated (dried grated) coconut, plus extra for sprinkling
225 g/8 oz/1 cup butter, at room temperature (you could also use a mixture of butter and coconut butter)
110 g/3¾ oz/½ cup caster (superfine) sugar
200 g/7 oz/1½ cups plain (all purpose) flour
100 g/3½ oz/1 cup cornflour (cornstarch)
a pinch of salt

Pairs well with
Limoncello

This is a great dessert recipe with a little twist: Sweet apricots combine with the more savoury elements of the ricotta and walnuts.

Place the apricot halves in a saucepan with the sugar, vanilla pod seeds and the dessert wine. Ensure the apricots are covered by the liquid; if not, top up with a little water. Place over a low-medium heat and bring the liquor up to a gentle simmer. Poach until the apricots are soft; this should take around 20 minutes. Remove the fruit from the liquor and set aside.

Continue to simmer the liquor to reduce it to the consistency of double (heavy) cream; this should take around 10 minutes.

To serve, arrange the apricot halves in serving bowls. Place spoonfuls of the ricotta around the apricots, then drizzle with the cooking liquor and honey. Scatter the crushed walnuts over the top and garnish with the lemon verbena leaves.

Serves 4

400 g/14 oz fresh apricots, halved and stoned (pitted)
2 tbsp caster (superfine) sugar
seeds from 1 vanilla pod (or ¼ tsp vanilla bean paste)
200 ml/7 fl oz/scant 1 cup Monbazillac or other sweet dessert wine
200 g/7 oz soft ricotta
1 tbsp truffle honey
3 tbsp crushed walnuts
10 lemon verbena leaves (or the leaves from 4 lemon thyme sprigs)

Pairs well with
Monbazillac

Poached Apricots with Ricotta, Truffle Honey and Walnuts

Affogato

This is the simplest of dessert recipes, but is perfect when you want something sweet but not too heavy. You can make it boozy or not boozy – tailor it to the mood! If you're feeling indecisive, then you can put a shot of coffee and a shot of alcohol in.

Take 4 teacups or small bowls and put a scoop of ice cream in each. Serve with the hot coffee/coffee liqueur/sherry in little jugs on the side. Pour the shot over the ice cream and eat! Yes, it is that simple. We like to dunk an amaretti biscuit in the melted ice cream as an extra treat.

Serves 4

4 scoops of good-quality ice cream (vanilla is the classic, but salted caramel also works well)
4 shots of either freshly made espresso coffee or coffee liqueur (we use Bepi Tosolini, but you can also use Tia Maria or Baileys Irish Cream) or Pedro Ximénez (or similar sweet sherry)
4 amaretti biscuits (cookies)

Banoffee Pot

As a kid, Rick went through a stage of making a banoffee pie every Sunday and then having it for breakfast every morning throughout the week. Needless to say, he was a little bigger then than he is now! It's always tricky cutting a banoffee pie into neat equal pieces, so we decided to put it into individual pots to make it easier to serve in the restaurant.

First make the caramel. Put the butter, sugar and double cream into a saucepan and melt over a medium heat. Bring to the boil and boil for 5 minutes, until the mixture has thickened slightly. Stir in the vanilla bean paste, then remove from the heat and set aside to cool.

Just before you are ready to serve, crumble 1–1½ digestive biscuits into the bottom of 4 small Kilner jars or short glasses. Spoon the cooled caramel over the crumbled biscuits. Slice the bananas and lay several pieces over the caramel layer. Whip the cream to stiff peaks and fold in the Greek yogurt, then spoon this mixture over the top of the bananas. Top with the chocolate curls and serve immediately, so the bananas don't brown.

Serves 4

100 g/3½ oz/7 tbsp unsalted butter
170 g/6 oz/generous ¾ cup soft light brown (light muscovado) sugar
125 ml/4 fl oz/½ cup double (heavy) cream
¼ tsp vanilla bean paste
4–6 digestive biscuits (graham crackers)
2 medium bananas
4 tbsp whipping cream
110 g/3¾ oz/½ cup Greek yogurt
dark chocolate curls or shavings, to decorate

Cornish Negroni

Put plenty of ice cubes into a cut-glass tumbler. Add your liquid ingredients, stir a few times and then finish off with orange zest or a slice of orange. Add more ice cubes, if needed.

50 ml/1½ fl oz/3 tbsp Tarquin's Cornish Gin (or ordinary gin)
25 ml/¾ fl oz/1½ tbsp Campari
25 ml/¾ fl oz/1½ tbsp Cocchi Vermouth di Torino (or ordinary red vermouth)
strip of orange zest or a slice of orange

Classic Margarita

Add all the ingredients, except for the salt, to a cocktail shaker filled with a handful of ice and shake well. Strain into a glass over ice cubes and then serve with a slice of lime. Salting the rim of the glass first is optional – depends on what your guest wants!

50 ml/1½ fl oz/3 tbsp tequila
25 ml/¾ fl oz/1½ tbsp Cointreau
a squeeze of agave nectar (syrup)
the juice of 1 lime, plus 1 lime cut into slices for garnish
salt, for the rim of the glass (optional)

Thai-style Bloody Mary

Put everything into a glass over ice, topping up with enough tomato juice to fill, and stir. Add a wedge of lime, a celery stick and a stripy straw.

Add an oyster on top, if required. Take the Tabasco sauce to the table, to serve, and guests can add more, to taste.

25 ml/¾ fl oz/1½ tbsp vodka
2 tsp lime juice
a few shakes of Worcestershire sauce, or to taste
finely diced fresh red chilli, to taste
½ tsp chopped coriander (cilantro)
tomato juice, to top up

To garnish:
a wedge of lime
a stick of celery
1 fresh oyster (optional)
a few drops of Tabasco sauce

Pinkster Gin and Tonic

Fill a glass with ice. Add the gin and raspberries, then 'clap' the mint leaves between your hands to release their aroma and add on top. Serve the tonic on the side for guests to serve themselves.

25 ml/¾ fl oz/1½ tbsp or 50 ml/
    1½ fl oz/3 tbsp Pinkster Gin
2 raspberries
5–6 mint leaves
tonic water, to taste

Kir Royale

Pour a small amount of cassis into a coupe glass, then fill to the top with prosecco or Cornish sparkling wine. Add a raspberry or an edible flower, to garnish.

a splash of crème de cassis
prosecco or Cornish sparkling wine
1 raspberry or edible flower

Dirty Oyster Martini

Add the vodka, dry martini and oyster juice to a cocktail shaker with a handful of ice and shake well. Strain into a martini glass, and serve with the oyster and a lemon wedge on the side.

75 ml/2¼ fl oz/4½ tbsp vodka
15 ml/½ fl oz/1 tbsp dry martini
the juice from 1 oyster, keeping the oyster itself for garnish
lemon wedge, for garnish

Baileys Espresso Martini

Make the shot of espresso coffee and let it cool a little.

Put the vodka and Baileys into a cocktail shaker with a handful of crushed ice, then add the cooled espresso and shake well. Strain into a prosecco glass or champagne coupe. Decorate with a coffee bean.

30 ml/1 fl oz/2 tbsp shot of espresso
25 ml/¾ fl oz/1½ tbsp vodka
50 ml/1½ fl oz/3 tbsp Baileys Irish Cream
coffee beans, for garnish

White Rabbit Fizz

Add the white port to a wine glass filled with plenty of ice, then pour in about two-thirds of the tonic. Garnish with the orange zest and add a straw. Serve with the rest of the tonic bottle on the side.

50 ml/1½ fl oz/3 tbsp White Rabbit dry white port
1 x 125 ml/4 fl oz tonic water bottle
a few large strips of orange zest

Fill a cocktail shaker with crushed ice and add all the ingredients. Shake well and then pour everything (including the ice) into a glass. Top up with more crushed ice, if needed, to serve.

50 ml/1½ fl oz/3 tbsp Sprizzato liqueur (Aperol can also be used)
juice of 1 lime
generous pinch of chopped coriander (cilantro)
generous pinch of chopped red chilli

Gamberi Sul Prato (Prawn on the Lawn)

Index

Suppliers

Scotland

Armstrong's of Stockbridge
80 Raeburn Place
Edinburgh EH4 1HH
www.armstrongsofstockbridge.co.uk

The Fish People
350 Scotland Street
Glasgow G5 8QF
www.thefishpeopleshop.co.uk

North East England

F.R. Fowler & Son
1 Gerard Avenue
Burnholme
York YO31 0QT
www.fowlersofyork.co.uk

Latimer's Seafood Ltd
Shell Hill
Bents Road
Whitburn
Sunderland SR6 7NT
www.latimers.com

Ramus Seafoods
Ocean House
Kings Road
Harrogate
North Yorkshire HG1 5HY
www.ramus.co.uk

Taylor Foods
19a Elm Road
West Chirton North Industrial Estate
North Shields NE29 8SE
www.taylorfoods.co.uk

North West England

Out of the Blue Fishmongers
484 Wilbraham Road
Chorlton-cum-Hardy
Manchester M21 9AS
www.outofthebluefish.co.uk

Wales

E. Ashton Fishmongers Ltd
Central Market
Cardiff CF10 1AU
www.ashtonfishmongers.co.uk

The Fabulous Fish Company
Newhall Farm Shop
Pwllmeyric
Chepstow
NP16 6LF
www.fabulousfish.co.uk

South West England

Field & Flower – online only
www.fieldandflower.co.uk

Fish for Thought
The Cornish Fish Store
Unit 1, Callywith Gate Business Park

Launceston Road
Bodmin
Cornwall PL31 2RQ
www.fishforthought.co.uk

New Wave Seafood
Units 3–6, 10–11 Horcott Industrial
   Estate
Fairford
Gloucestershire GL7 4BX
www.new-wave.co.uk

Prawn on the Lawn
11 Duke Street
Padstow
Cornwall PL28 8AB
www.prawnonthelawn.com

The Cornish Fishmonger
Wing of St Mawes Ltd
Unit 4
Warren Road
Indian Queens Industrial Estate
Indian Queens TR9 6TL
www. thecornishfishmonger.co.uk

South East England

M&J Seafoods
3–5 Faraday Road
Rabans Lane Industrial Estate
Aylesbury HP19 8RY
www.mjseafood.com

The Fish Society
Fish Palace
Coopers Place
Godalming GU8 5TG
www.thefishsociety.co.uk

Veasey & Sons Fishmongers
17 Hartfield Road
Forest Row
East Sussex RH18 5DN
www.veaseyandsons.co.uk

London

Elias Fish
8 Bittacy Hill
Mill Hill
London NW7 1LB
www.eliasfish.co.uk

Faircatch – box scheme for South-
   West Londoners
80 Geraldine Road
London SW18 2NL
www.faircatch.co.uk

Fin and Flounder
71 Broadway Market
London Fields
Hackney
London E8 4PH
www.finandflounder.co.uk

Moxon's
Locations in Clapham South, South
   Kensington, East Dulwich and
   Islington
www.moxonsfreshfish.com

Prawn on the Lawn
292–294 St.Pauls Road
London N1 2LH
www.prawnonthelawn.com

The Chelsea Fishmonger
10 Cale Street
Chelsea
London SW3 3QU
www.thechelseafishmonger.co.uk

- WINKLES, GARLIC BUTER KE
- SQUID, N'DUJA, TARRAGO
- RAY WING, WILD GARLIC, FE
- BURRATA, CRISPY ARTICHOKE
- SZECHUAN PRAWNS £8.5

- BABY GEM, TRUFFLE OIL, 6/
- TOMATO + TARRAGON SALA
- HOME MADE SODA BREAD

Acknowledgements

There are so many people to thank for getting us to the point of publishing our first book. We'd love to dedicate this book to everyone who has helped along the way. If we've forgotten anyone, we're sorry, but we love you and are so grateful for everything!

Firstly, thanks to our parents, grandparents, my bros, Will and Harry, and cousin Will, who have been amazing in all areas of POTL and our lives in general – we couldn't have done any of this without you.

To all our friends, those who've helped both in the restaurant and out, who've put up with us missing important occasions, and listened to us talk relentlessly about the restaurant and still chosen to hang out with us despite everything!

To our awesome staff, past and present, who work day in, day out, to carry out our vision for what the POTL experience should be. We're so grateful for all of your hard work, and we love working with each and every one of you. Daniela and Patrizia, thank you so much for your amazing work keeping the Islington restaurant running as if we were there ourselves – you guys are awesome. Rob, for all your help getting Padstow up and running and for helping us get it to where we are today, thank you.

To Jamie, for cycling past the butchers and texting me a pic of the 'to let' sign, which became the home of the first POTL, and to Reg, our landlord in Islington, who gave us the opportunity to start our dream, we can't thank you enough.

To our suppliers, who have provided us with the best ingredients over the years, I hope we do your products justice. Special mention to the Murts, Wild Harbour, Tim and Luke at Rock Shellfish, Rupert and Louis (South Coast Fisheries), Ross Geach (Padstow Kitchen Garden), Pete (Padstow Shellfish Co.), Liz and Engin (Trevibban Mill), Des and Caron (Padstow Brewing Co.) and Wright Bros.

To Mitch Tonks, for the foreword to the book, for being our inspiration and someone for whom we have a huge amount of respect – thank you so much for all your support.

To Tim and Alison (Sommelier's Choice), thank you for providing us with wicked wines, more support than we could imagine and all the awesome wine recommendations throughout the book.

To Paul and Emma Ainsworth and the team, for being so welcoming when we first came to Padstow. I had an incredible experience working in your kitchen. Thank you.

To all the guys at Pavilion and Emily Preece-Morrison, who believed in what we do, and gave us this opportunity to put together our favourite recipes to share with everyone, thanks for coping with us missing nearly every single deadline!

Finally, to Steven Joyce, Oliver Rowe, Lizzie Kamenetzky and Linda Berlin for the wicked pics throughout the book. We had so much fun with you and all the team – negronis on the beach at 8am should be mandatory!

Rick and Katie